90 Days with
THE GOD
WHO speaks

B&H
PUBLISHING GROUP

NASHVILLE, TENNESSEE

Published by B&H Publishing Group
Nashville, Tennessee

Content has been developed from *The Gospel Project™: Adult Leader Guide*, copyright 2012 by LifeWay Christian Resources, Nashville, Tennessee. Used by permission.

1 2 3 4 5 6 7 • 21 20 19 18 17

Contents

God speaks. From the beginning of time and in the pages of Scripture, God reveals Himself as a God who speaks. His speech is a demonstration of His power, grace, and authority. Because of this truth, there is nothing more important in life than hearing from God and obeying His voice.

Introduction

This devotional has been created out of the content in The Gospel Project curriculum. The curriculum was developed to fulfill the need churches have expressed for theologically driven curriculum that is biblical and accessible. This devotional gives an opportunity for individuals to reflect through the material in a 90-day devotional style. Through it you will develop an overall view of the Bible in light of the gospel of Jesus Christ.

While this devotional was developed to go through daily, use it in the way that is most conductive to your study of the Bible. That might mean doing one devotional per day, alternating with another form study, once a week when you have time, or even ten in one day.

Open your heart, and allow God to show you the truth of Scripture, and the story of His Son, Jesus Christ.

Day 1

Let's Start with the Big Picture

 In the beginning, the all-powerful, personal God created the universe. This God created human beings in His image to live joyfully in His presence, in humble submission to His gracious authority. But all of us have rebelled against God and, in consequence, must suffer the punishment of our rebellion: physical death and the wrath of God.

Thankfully, God initiated a rescue plan, which began with His choosing the nation of Israel to display His glory in a fallen world. The Bible describes how God acted mightily on Israel's behalf, rescuing His people from slavery and then giving them His holy law. But God's people—like all of us—failed to rightly reflect the glory of God.

Then, in the fullness of time, in the Person of Jesus Christ, God Himself came to renew the world and restore His people. Jesus perfectly obeyed the law given to Israel. Though innocent, He suffered the consequences of human rebellion by His death on a cross. But three days later, God raised Him from the dead.

Now the church of Jesus Christ has been commissioned by God to take the news of Christ's work to the world. Empowered by God's Spirit, the church calls all people everywhere to repent of sin and to trust in Christ alone for our forgiveness. Repentance and faith restores our relationship with God and results in a life of ongoing transformation.

The Bible promises that Jesus Christ will return to this earth as the conquering King. Only those who live in repentant faith in Christ will escape God's judgment and live joyfully in God's presence for all eternity.

God's message is the same to all of us: repent and believe, before it is too late. Confess with your mouth that Jesus is Lord and believe with your heart that God raised Him from the dead, and you will be saved.

Throughout this study we are going to take a look at the different attributes of God, specifically how He communicates with us. The thing you need to remember every single day is that everything points back to the gospel. Today may be labeled Day 1, but it is really the foundational day. It is the day you can go back and read when you find yourself with a few extra minutes. It is the day you can look back to when you find yourself deep in the Scripture and you need to pull back and see the big picture story that God has written for us.

Do you ever have trouble seeing the
big picture of the gospel?

Pray that God will use these 90 days to open your eyes
to the Truth of the gospel and draw you closer to Him.

DAY 2

Is Communication Important?

 Helen Keller was only nineteen months when a childhood illness left her deaf and blind, a prisoner to a world of inexpressible thoughts. Years later, Helen Keller's parents hired a teacher, Anne Sullivan, who sought to break into the six-year-old's world of silent darkness. Sullivan's breakthrough came when she taught Helen how to sign the word *water*. Helen described the moment she first realized that her teacher was communicating with her:

> *Someone was drawing water and my teacher placed my hand under the spout. As the cool stream gushed over one hand she spelled into the other the word water, first slowly, then rapidly. I stood still, my whole attention fixed upon the motions of her fingers. Suddenly I felt a misty consciousness as of something forgotten—a thrill of returning thought; and somehow the mystery of language was revealed to me.*[1]

The story of Helen Keller reminds us of the power of communication. In our wired world of iPhones and iPads, Facebook and Skype, we take for granted the ease of communication. We've grown accustomed to receiving a

---

1. Helen Keller, *The Story of My Life* (Middlesex: The Echo Library, 2007), 13–14.

constant stream of information. The privilege of being personally addressed is overshadowed by the commonness of constant communication with family and friends. Communication is common in the way that breathing and sleeping are common. Communicating is an important aspect of human existence, so much so that we consider it to be particularly harrowing to suffer from a disease that takes away a person's ability to communicate, especially when the mind is left intact.

Some people view human interaction as so vital to human flourishing that they protest the practice of placing prisoners in solitary confinement for an extended period of time believing that complete solitude destroys the mental and relational capacities of an individual.

Regardless of one's view of the legitimacy of solitary confinement, it's fascinating that this kind of debate would even take place. The discussion itself demonstrates the importance of verbal interaction for human flourishing. We are relational beings. We were made for words.

No wonder the first chapter of the Bible focuses on the God who speaks. The first inspired words God spoke to us in the Bible are about Him speaking! This emphasis that God placed on communication should remind us of our need to hear from God. Without God choosing to reveal Himself to us, we would be like Helen Keller—deaf and blind to the reality of the world we live in. Without God's revelation, we would be unaware of His expectations for us and of His provision for salvation.

Why do you think God designed humans with an innate need to communicate? What does this design communicate about the nature and desire of God?

The God Who Speaks Has Authority

In the beginning God created the heavens and the earth. Now the earth was formless and empty, darkness covered the surface of the watery depths, and the Spirit of God was hovering over the surface of the waters. Then God said, "Let there be light," and there was light. (Gen. 1:1–3)

 Notice the power of God's word in this passage. With just two words spoken by God, light came into existence. God created by *speaking*. He spoke the world into existence. And the result of His speaking demonstrates how powerful His speech is.

Words change things. When a pastor stands next to a gushing groom and a beaming bride and says, "I now pronounce you husband and wife," their status changes. They become united before God and God's people. They are ushered into the union of holy matrimony. The spoken word changed them forever because it was spoken with authority. But words have no authority in themselves. Words are only powerful when spoken by someone with power.

Responding to the powerful nature of God's speech, the psalmist praised God for His creative authority: "Praise

Him, sun and moon; praise Him, all you shining stars. Praise Him, highest heavens, and you waters above the heavens. Let them praise the name of Yahweh, for He commanded, and they were created" (Ps. 148:3–5).

Words matter. Words carry weight. And the weightiest words are those uttered by the most glorious Being in the universe. His words matter because of who He is. The truth that God speaks is what separates Him from all idols. In the Old Testament, we see frequent showdowns between the true God of Israel and the false gods of pagan peoples. Whether it be the plagues God sent on Egypt (corresponding with the Egyptian gods; Exod. 7–12) or Elijah calling down fire on Mount Carmel (after the prophets of Baal cried out in vain; 1 Kings 18), the writers of the Bible delight in showing the power of God over idolatry. In Psalm 115:3–5, we read: "Our God is in heaven and does whatever He pleases. Their idols are silver and gold, made by human hands. They have mouths but cannot speak, eyes, but cannot see." The contrast is clear. God is Spirit. He has no physical mouth, and yet He speaks. The idols, on the other hand, are physical. They have mouths but are silent. God alone has authority. God is the God who speaks.

In what ways does the impact of a word of encouragement or criticism change depending upon the source?

How does our belief that God has spoken affect our view of Scripture? The world we live in? Our day-to-day behavior?

DAY 4

The God Who Speaks Is
Merciful to Reveal Himself to Us

 In Exodus 3:2–6, we are given a glimpse of how God revealed Himself to Moses in the form of a burning bush.

Then the Angel of the LORD appeared to him in a flame of fire within a bush. As Moses looked, he saw that the bush was on fire but was not consumed. So Moses thought: I must go over and look at this remarkable sight. Why isn't the bush burning up? When the LORD saw that he had gone over to look, God called out to him from the bush, "Moses, Moses!" "Here I am," he answered. "Do not come closer," He said. "Remove the sandals from your feet, for the place where you are standing is holy ground." Then He continued, "I am the God of your father, the God of Abraham, the God of Isaac, and the God of Jacob." Moses hid his face because he was afraid to look at God.

This account shows us that mercy is at the heart of God's revelation to us. Notice who initiated the conversation. God is the One who came to Moses. He mercifully revealed Himself and then identified Himself as the God of Moses' forefathers. Humans have no right to demand an audience with God. God is not accountable to us; we are accountable to Him. God would have been fully just and righteous to create this world and leave it to natural processes, never to intervene, never to communicate with His human creatures, and never to involve Himself with our human plight. There is nothing about our existence that forces God to be a God who reveals Himself. And yet God speaks.

It is also an act of grace that God would reveal Himself to us personally. God was under no obligation to pull back the curtain and let us see aspects of His character and evidences of His power. He could have spoken the world into existence and then never spoken again, leaving us in ignorance about our Creator and our purpose. In fact, some people hold to a worldview that imagines this very scenario. (And some Christians who don't believe this way still live this way!) Deism teaches that God created the world much like a clockmaker puts together a clock. But then the Deist god no longer intervenes in our affairs. He lets the clock begin to tick, and then he steps back and becomes uninvolved.

In Deuteronomy 4:33, Moses reminded the Israelites of the great privilege they had received in hearing the voice of God. He asked, "Has a people heard God's voice speaking from the fire as you have, and lived?" The rhetorical effect of Moses' question demonstrated the mercy that comes from hearing God speak. The fact that God would choose to reveal Himself, and to do so in such a way as to allow us to live, is an act of mercy.

Here we see the good news of the gospel! The gospel is the story of a God who issues a call to helpless sinners. In our blindness and deafness, we are imprisoned by our own sinfulness. We cannot see the goodness of God until He gives us new eyes. We cannot hear the voice of God until

He opens our ears. Like Helen Keller, we struggle to make sense of the world around us—why we are here and where we are going. But God—out of sheer grace—chose to enter our world of darkness through the Person of Jesus Christ.

In His perfect life and sacrificial death, Jesus revealed God to us. He showed us God's character. He demonstrated the love at the heart of the Father's authority. God created us out of mercy. He has spoken to us out of mercy. He became one of us out of His mercy. And He calls us to Himself out of His mercy. Just as Anne Sullivan broke through to Helen, the Holy Spirit opens the eyes of our heart so we can see His goodness and His glory and respond with gratitude. Thinking about "the God who speaks" is not merely an intellectual exercise. Revelation is more than a doctrine about the inspiration of the Scriptures. It is more than a doctrine about the beauty of God's creation. Revelation is at the very heart of what God has done on our behalf to bring Himself glory. As New Testament scholar Klyne Snodgrass has said, "Revelation does not merely bring the gospel: the gospel is revelation."

If it is true that God's revelation demonstrates His authority and His mercy, what should be our response to others? What else do we learn about this God who has spoken?

DAY 5

The God Who Speaks
Gives Us Tasks

 If it is true that God has spoken, then there is nothing greater we can do than listen to what our Creator has said. What might be some of the reasons people don't want to believe that God has spoken?

Once we recognize the authority of the God who speaks and the mercy from which He speaks, we are then responsible to lovingly obey God's commands. The command has been issued. What will our response be?

In Genesis 1:27–30, God told the first humans, Adam and Eve, what He expected of them.

So God created man in His own image; He created him in the image of God; He created them male and female. God blessed them, and God said to them, "Be fruitful, multiply, fill the earth, and subdue it. Rule the fish of the sea, the birds of the sky, and every creature that crawls the earth." God also said, "Look, I have given you every seed-bearing plant on the surface of the entire earth and every tree whose fruit contains seed. This food will be for you, for all the wildlife of the earth, for every bird of the sky, and for every creature that crawls on the earth—everything having the breath of life in it. I have given every green plant for food." And it was so.

Notice the progression again: God created (authority); then He blessed (mercy). Finally, He gave tasks. Out of His authority, God created Adam and Eve. Out of His mercy, He blessed them. Then God's mercy led to His tasking Adam and Eve with cultivating His good creation. Why do you think it is important that we understand this progression? What might happen if we seek to understand the task apart from God's blessing?

Too many times we get the order backwards. We begin with the tasks of the Christian life and seek to receive God's blessing as a result of our obedience. But the gospel turns these expectations upside down. God first blesses His children. Only then does He task them with ruling wisely over the earth.

This pattern is seen in other places in Scripture as well. God first delivered the children of Israel from their slavery in Egypt. Then He gave them the law on Mount Sinai. In the New Testament, Christ died for our sins and rose again to new life, saving us from our sins. Then He reminded us of His authority as He commissioned us to take the gospel to all nations. When we begin with the task rather than the blessing, we cut ourselves off from the very power that is necessary to fulfill the tasks God has given us. The blessing of the gospel—the gift of undeserved grace—should motivate and drive our obedience. As we embrace the gospel, the gospel then empowers our love for God and for our neighbor.

When we begin with our obedience instead of God's blessing, we invert the gospel. We begin to think that we can somehow put God in our debt. If we only do enough good works, maybe God will bless us. This is humanity's futile attempt at keeping control. We'd rather think that God owes us. As long as we think someone owes us, we maintain a sense of control. Grace—in contrast—is scary! When we come to understand that accomplishing our task is made possible only because of God's initial blessing of grace, then there is nothing God can't ask of us. There is nothing He owes us. We owe Him everything—our very lives.

What are the areas in your life where you have inverted the gospel?

What are the ways that God has blessed you before you were given a task?

DAY 6

Why Does God Teach Us to Speak?

 After Anne Sullivan was able to communicate with Helen Keller, she began to teach her how to communicate with others. Anne did not speak to Helen in order to become merely a companion to her. Anne saw Helen's potential for communication. Helen Keller became an author and activist in later years. The power of that initial moment of communication led to places no one would have imagined. So it is with us. God does not speak to us so that we might keep Him company or that we might merely be friends. He speaks to us and lavishes the grace of His salvation upon us so that we might then get to work accomplishing all that He has called us to do. The God who speaks is the God who gives tasks. God communicates His commands, and then He breathes His Spirit into our hearts, enabling us to learn, live, and love.

Has God spoken to you through His Word in the past few months? What Scripture passages has God used to speak to you?

What blessings have you received from God in the past few months?

What tasks has God presented to you as a result of these blessings?

God Is Not Hiding

In the 1998 film *The Truman Show*, Jim Carrey plays Truman Burbank, a generally cheerful insurance adjuster in a cozy island town whose days run like clockwork—until the day a stage light falls out of the heavens and crashes near his car. Though the news on the radio says an airplane has been shedding parts, Truman begins to develop a suspicious awareness that everything is not as it seems:

- A technical difficulty on his car stereo broadcasts the very route he is driving.
- A homeless man calling his name on the street looks very much like the father he thought was dead.
- An elevator in an office building opens to reveal what looks like a backstage area.

As Truman begins paying attention to the world around him, he discovers he is the unwitting star of a reality television show. Everyone in his life is an actor; all the people he sees throughout the day are extras; and the island town he lives in is actually a gigantic set overseen by a television director with a God complex. As Truman begins looking back through his life and at the world around him, he realizes the clues to reality were there all along. *The Truman Show* is just a movie, of course (although its human-in-a-bubble premise doesn't seem so strange in these days of strange reality

15

television shows!), but it is nevertheless a good metaphor for how billions of people live their lives in this world every day. They wake up, go about their routines, and go to bed, only to start the ritual all over again.

Sometimes they suspect the world around them is trying to tell them something about itself and what's outside of it, but they fail over and over again to put those clues together. They are like a person who finds a watch on the sidewalk and assumes it is the natural result of millions of years of sand, wind, and sun.

The movie is a good metaphor for how billions of people live their lives: seeing the signs in daily life (the sun's rising, the sea's swelling, the changing of the seasons, the clockwork of the solar system, the intricacies of DNA) as peeks behind the stage. We find that watch on the sidewalk and know it didn't arrive there accidentally. It was dropped, it was owned, and before all that, it was made. The world is telling us something; we just know it!

It's telling us something about itself, about us, and about what's behind it all. But what? What is it saying?

According to the Bible, the world around us is testifying to all that there is a Creator. Furthermore, the world around us is telling us what the Creator is like, and something of His plans. We call this reality general revelation because it refers to the general way God reveals Himself to people everywhere.

What are some of the hints and clues we see in creation that point us to the existence of a Creator? Conversely, what are some of the aspects of creation that cause some people to believe that no Creator exists?

DAY 8

God Reveals His Existence through Creation

 One of the most direct references to general revelation we find in the Scriptures is Psalm 19:1–6.

The heavens declare the glory of God, and the sky proclaims the work of His hands. Day after day they pour out speech; night after night they communicate knowledge. There is no speech; there are no words; their voice is not heard. Their message has gone out to all the earth, and their words to the ends of the world. . . . It is like a groom coming from the bridal chamber; it rejoices like an athlete running a course. It rises from one end of the heavens and circles to their other end; nothing is hidden from its heat.

According to this passage, the created world is constantly saying something about its Creator—or more accurately, the Creator is constantly saying something about Himself through His created world. The picture we receive from the psalmist is of a world that acts as a loudspeaker, a stage, and an art gallery—all pointing to God's glory. The sky proclaims that all this work has a Designer's hands behind it.

Just like the presence of a watch on a sidewalk indicates a watchmaker, our finely tuned bodies living in this finely tuned world hanging in this finely tuned cosmos point to the logical existence of a Creator. Nobody looks at a Mercedes Benz, for example, and assumes there was an explosion at a junkyard. According to the direct revelation of Psalm 19:1–6, the heavens (and the sky) are every day "pouring out speech" and every night "communicating knowledge" that God exists.

The sense we receive in verses 1–2 is of continual revelation. Creation never presses "pause" on its proclaiming that it is an effect, not a cause, and that it has an Originator. Verse 3 can be difficult to sort out, but the context of the passage gives us two most likely interpretations.

The first is that despite the nonstop speech and communication, some people simply ignore it as if it doesn't exist; the voice is not heard. Nevertheless, they cannot say they were not told, only that they did not listen. It is for a similar reason that Jesus, borrowing from Isaiah 6:9–10, says this in Matthew 13:15 of those people hardened to His message: "For this people's heart has grown callous; their ears are hard of hearing, and they have shut their eyes; otherwise they might see with their eyes and hear with their ears, understand with their hearts and turn back—and I would cure them."

The second possible interpretation of Psalm 19:3 is simply that David is noting the nature of general revelation, which is to say, it is not a speech that comes in an audible voice or literal words. The communication and knowledge is proclaimed, but not in the direct way that special revelation is. A watch tells us it has a watchmaker, but not in the same way as does shaking the watchmaker's hand and hearing his voice say, "I made that."

Both of these senses are true of Psalm 19:3. It is true that creation is proclaiming its Creator, but many either don't hear it or they hear it but reject it. It is also true that the way creation proclaims its Creator is not as direct as the way the Creator proclaims Himself.

In any event, verse 4 tells us that the "message has gone out to all the earth, and their words to the ends of the world." In other words, no place is absent general revelation. Nature's "music" points us to look for the Conductor. Nature's beauty points us to look for the Artist. The vastness of the Sahara Desert and the Arctic tundra and the mighty oceans, in making us feel small and vulnerable, point us to God, the strong Tower.

But the general revelation in the created order of the universe doesn't just tell us that there is a God, it tells us something about that God. To borrow a phrase from C. S. Lewis, general revelation doesn't merely tell us a God exists, it tells us this God exists. Psalm 19:1 tells us "The heavens declare the glory of God," not merely the presence of God. The word *glory* has the sense of "weightiness" or "worth." God's glory is the sum impression of all that God is. What we learn first about God from His general revelation is that God will not settle for being acknowledged. He wants to be known! So there is something about the heavens—their vastness, their beauty, their complexity, their power, their impression upon little ol' us—that tells us something about Him.

Think about the ways people attempt to guard themselves from God's revelation. What are some of the most common ways we try to hide from God's voice and drown it out?

God Reveals His Attributes through Creation

 Suppose you came home one day to find a package with this note attached: "These are the personal effects of your twin brother Joe, recently deceased." Once you got over the initial shock of discovering you had a twin brother you never knew about, you'd open the package and look at the contents, hoping they might tell you something about this brother.

If the package contained a leather jacket, a set of brass knuckles, and some cigarettes, that wouldn't tell you everything about your brother, but it would certainly give you a general impression, wouldn't it? The package's existence would tell you that you had a brother, but the package's contents would tell you a bit about him.

In the same way, the created world tells us we have a God, and what we see in the created world tells us some general things about Him. By seeing the general revelation of "the heavens" and the rest of the world, we can get a sense of God's glory, the sum of His attributes.

In Romans 1:20, Paul writes:

For His invisible attributes, that is, His eternal power and divine nature, have been clearly seen since the

creation of the world, being understood through what
He has made. As a result, people are without excuse.

Nobody can rightfully say, "I never heard the gospel message contained in the Bible, so I am not responsible for my own sin," because there is enough evidence of God's sovereign rule (over both people and their sin) in general revelation that nobody can say they weren't directed to seek Him out in special revelation.

Again, we should repeat that general revelation does not tell us all there is to know about God, nor can we hear the specific gospel message of salvation in the declarations of the heavens. Still, enough is communicated that "people are without excuse." Paul says the visible world reveals God's invisible attributes, namely, His "eternal power and divine nature." God's "eternal power" can have two meanings. The first is that God's power is without end or limit. This is an affirmation of His omnipotence.

We see God's eternal power revealed through the vastness of the cosmos and through the mighty forces at work in nature. The expanse of space or the unfathomable depths of the ocean ought to humble mankind. The same is true of an eruption of a volcano or the strength of a tsunami. These shows of power give us an otherworldly and overwhelming sense of being in the presence of the divine Being. As Matt Chandler has said while preaching, "Nobody stands at the base of the Rocky Mountains and says, 'Remember that time I benched 300 pounds in high school?'"

What does the complexity and variety
of nature tell us about God?

God Reveals His Divine Nature through Creation

We see that God's power upholds eternity when we really begin to ponder the clock-like order of the universe. The planets are precisely aligned for Earth's specialness. The conditions on Earth are precisely balanced for life. The chemicals in human life are precisely proportioned for growth, intelligence, and creativity. Also, despite the destructive forces of tornadoes, hurricanes, earthquakes, lightning, tsunamis, floods, volcanic eruptions, and asteroids falling from the sky, this place keeps on keeping on. If we cannot see the sustaining power of God's providential care in creation's endurance, we likely will not see it in the pages of Scripture.

How is God's "divine nature" revealed through what we see? One of the clearest imprints is not just in the way we search for objects to worship but is right here inside, in the way we think and act. We read in Genesis 1:27: "So God created man in His own image; He created him in the image of God; He created them male and female."

Because we are creatures made in God's image, we have innate senses and compulsions that point to the reality of God's divine nature. Of course, we are not divine ourselves, and after the fall of mankind, the image of God in us is obscured and broken. Still, we can nevertheless see that mankind's generally innate sense of justice and fairness, compulsion to create, ability to express and experience love, and frequent appeals to conscience all point away from our being the evolved result of a random electric current in a primordial goop.

If you listen to children playing long enough, you will eventually hear the recurring cry, "That's not fair!" While we all have a moral compass that's skewed in the wiring due to sin, we still have an innate sense of right and wrong, just and unjust, fair and unfair. Apart from the Spirit's discipline, it is impossible for us to apply these impulses in selfless ways, but the presence of them to begin with indicates an ultimate right and an ultimate justice. Thanks to special revelation, we know that this is found in our perfectly holy and just God.

Name some of God's attributes revealed in the Bible. How might some of these be communicated in the visible world? Where and how do we see them proclaimed in nature, including in general human experience?

God Reveals His Intentions through Creation

There is yet another message we receive in general revelation. The visible world tells us that there is a God as well as something about what God is like, but the visible world still further tells us something about God's plans.

In Acts 14, Barnabas and Paul are in Lystra when a priest of Zeus begins to lead a crowd in making sacrifices to them. Barnabas and Paul, in dramatic fashion, interrupt the proceedings, tear their clothes, and proclaim to the crowd:

> *Men! Why are you doing these things? We are men also, with the same nature as you, and we are proclaiming good news to you, that you should turn from these worthless things to the living God, who made the heaven, the earth, the sea, and everything in them. In past generations He allowed all the nations to go their own way, although He did not leave Himself without a witness, since He did what is good by giving you rain from heaven and fruitful seasons and satisfying your hearts with food and happiness.*

As the pagan demand for more sacrifices to a dead god continued, Barnabas and Paul desperately wanted these people to know the good news that Jesus has made the sacrifice to end all sacrifices, and He did so to honor the will of a Heavenly Father who had been far better to the unsaved people of Lystra than Zeus had been. The missionaries pointed to the evidence: "You have a witness that this is true!" they cried. "He has given you rain and harvest and good food and happiness."

The brokenness we see in "the whole creation," then, is signaling to us that (a) something is wrong and (b) there is something better.

In this way, when natural disasters occur and when societies undergo discord, we are pushed to hope for something better, which is in itself an arrow pointing toward the "something better" God intends to do. Acts 14:17 and Romans 8:22 give us the imprint of the gospel story!

Looking at the world around us, we recognize that this place is broken, but there is pleasure to be had. This is the concept of "common grace," which we also see in Matthew 5:45: "For He causes His sun to rise on the evil and the good, and sends rain on the righteous and the unrighteous." The benevolent heart of God is made visible through common grace. God intends for the happiness we experience in marriage, parenting, and His other good gifts to point us back to Him. The gifts everyone enjoys in this life lead to the Giver. Yet not everyone has eyes to see.

What does the description of the actions of Paul and Barnabas in Acts 14:11–18 tell us about evangelistic motives, demeanor, strategy, and message?

God's General Revelation

 The general revelation we receive in the created world displays the Giver's fingerprints everywhere, and these prints tell us something of His intentions. We cannot receive the gospel message in general revelation, but we can certainly sense its echoes. Things like the metamorphosis of the butterfly can help us illustrate Christ's death, burial, and resurrection—and ours in response. Even the cycle of the seasons—from the death of winter to the newness of spring—helps us see the imprint of the gospel.

The Reformers thought of the world as a grand theater in which God showcases His glory. One thing we must say about this theater, of course, is that it is not itself the story but the stage for it. Like a good stage set, it tells us something of the story before the players even enter and begin reciting their lines. But it is the script that really reveals.

In *Mere Christianity*, C. S. Lewis tells of the time an old Air Force officer interrupted his talk on religion to say: "I'm a religious man too. I know there's a God. I've felt Him: out alone in the desert at night: the tremendous mystery. And that's just why I don't believe all your neat little dogmas and formulas about Him. To anyone who's met the real thing they all seem so petty and pedantic and unreal!"

Lewis goes on to honor the man's experience of "feeling God's presence" out in the wilderness of nature, but he denies the sufficiency of that sort of experience. He writes: "You see, what happened to that man in the desert may have been real, and was certainly exciting, but nothing comes of it. It leads nowhere. There is nothing to do about it. In fact, that is just why a vague religion—all about feeling God in nature, and so on— is so attractive. It is all thrills and no work; like watching the waves from the beach. But you will not get to Newfoundland by studying the Atlantic that way, and you will not get eternal life by simply feeling the presence of God in flowers or music."

Thankfully, while God does communicate His presence, His attributes, and His intentions through the gift of general revelation, He wants to be even clearer than that.

What are some other general revelation "signposts" we find in creation that illustrate the gospel of Jesus' life, death, and resurrection?

Why is it wrong to think that "experiencing God" in nature is enough?

How will the truth of general revelation help or otherwise affect your mission to be a witness to the gospel of Jesus?

Day 13

God Is Not Mute

 We have considered general revelation—the way in which God reveals Himself to us through His creation. Imagine you are walking along a sidewalk and discover a wristwatch on the ground. When you pick it up to examine it, would you deduce that it was the random result of an explosion in a metal and glass factory? Would you assume from its design and precision that it had come into being purely by accident, the fortuitous result of some minor cataclysm? Perhaps you know a little about science, and while some scientists argue that highly developed organization does result from disorganized material "naturally," you know that the second law of thermodynamics states that natural things actually are constantly breaking down. So that wristwatch could not have assembled itself out of dust, and if you left that wristwatch on the ground for a billion years, it would not turn into Big Ben but to dirt. What do you assume then?

You assume the watch was made on purpose. Some outside, intelligent force used the means at its disposal to gather or manufacture the materials, to design the internal mechanism and the external display, and to put it all together so that—voila!—the watch was made. To the logical mind, the watch reveals the existence of a watchmaker.

As in the general revelation of God's glory in creation, the watch may reveal some things about its maker, that he has a keen eye, that he has an expert hand, and the like. These characteristics are clearly evident. They tell us things we ought to know about the maker's existence and his character. But all of the things the watch tells us about its maker have to be deduced. And they don't tell us some of the most critical things about the watchmaker—his name, for instance.

Thankfully, God has not left us to deduce all we need to know from His general revelation in creation alone. He also gets straight to the point by providing what we call special revelation. Special revelation is different from general revelation because it refers to the way God reveals specific things about Himself and His plan for the created world—including us—in His written Word. The general revelation of creation is reflecting God's glory, but in the special revelation of the Bible, God is proclaiming His glory Himself.

How does how God reveals Himself in Scripture differ from how He reveals Himself in creation?

Day 14

God Is the Author of Scripture

 Though the Bible has approximately forty different authors, runs the gamut of history to law, prophecy to poetry, and includes sixty-six books written over the span of sixteen hundred years, it has one Author who made every word sure and every truth proclaimed.

Paul reminds Timothy of this vital truth in 2 Timothy 3:16–17:

> *All Scripture is inspired by God and is profitable for teaching, for rebuking, for correcting, for training in righteousness, so that the man of God may be complete, equipped for every good work.*

This short passage reveals to us a few things about itself and every other verse in the Bible. First, it tells us that every word of Scripture comes from God Himself, that they are "inspired" by the Holy Spirit. But what does this sort of inspiration mean?

When we say God inspired men to write the Bible, we don't mean it in the same way that a man may write a poem because he was inspired by a beautiful woman or a waterfall. The inspiration that the Holy Spirit provided in revealing the Word of God was direct, not indirect.

On the other hand, the inspiration that the Spirit provided in the revelation of the Word of God did not turn the human authors into automatic dictation machines. They weren't possessed—at least not in the sense of losing control over their own faculties. God used men to write the Bible, but He did so without overriding their personalities.

When Paul taught that his biblical words were inspired by God, he meant that God took whatever care determined necessary to make sure that what Paul and all the other biblical writers said was what God wanted said.

Second Timothy 3:16–17 also tells us that because all Scripture is authored by God, all Scripture has authority. This is implicitly evident in the acknowledgment that through the Bible the sovereign God of the universe is declaring and commanding. But it is explicitly evident in the way Paul tells Timothy that the Word of God contains all that we need to be "complete" and "equipped for every good work." And since the Bible's help for us in these areas is comprehensive and exclusive, it is therefore authoritative.

We should neither need nor want to look outside of the Bible to find out what God deems as "need to know" knowledge. And because the Bible is authoritative in this way, we don't need experiential wisdom to authenticate it or supplement it.

What does the truth that God chose not to override the personalities of the Bible's authors say about our own personalities? In what ways can God use our circumstances and personalities in our proclamation of His truth?

In what ways might Christians be tempted to supplement the Bible's authority with something else?

God Gives Scripture Authority

In recent years, we've seen a number of books chronicling near-death experiences and visits to heaven and back. Depending on your perspective, these recollections are delightfully encouraging or dubious and discard-worthy.

But we can observe in the popularity of "visiting heaven books" a troubling sentiment about the Bible. Setting aside for the moment whether the stories in those books actually happened and the extra-biblical innovation some of them reveal (people who go to heaven get wings, according to some), it appears that for many Christians such books "prove" the truth of the Scriptures. "See?" many say, "the Bible is true after all! This person went to heaven and back."

But we don't need people outside the Bible to tell us that. The words inside the Bible tell us that quite plainly. Similarly, the excitement generated by these books, as if they somehow authenticate the Christian worldview and the narrative of the gospel, can reveal a lack of confidence in the Bible itself, which is authenticated and authoritative all on its own.

The Bible doesn't need our fantastic experiences to verify it. It is the very Word of God from the very breath of God. One complication we often miss in the modern fantastic tales of heavenly adventure is that the hero tends to be the teller of the story. It is not always wrong to celebrate human achievement, of course, but as it pertains to spiritual things, it is clear that the hero of the Bible's story is not man but God Himself. God is the major Actor in the grand, biblical epic. Even the mightiest and cleverest of men in the Bible are revealed to be sinful, broken servants to our glorious God. And everything God reveals in the Bible is meant to amplify His own glory.

This means that while the Bible is a message for us, it is ultimately a message about God. All that God does in the great history of redemption He does chiefly for His own renown.

Do you agree with the statement "In all God does, His first aim is to glorify Himself"? Why or why not? What are some ways that God's glorifying Himself is a benefit to us?

Day 16

God Clearly Reveals His Expectations for Humanity

 While general revelation reveals there is a God to know, special revelation reveals that God wants to be known personally.

We surveyed Psalm 19:1–6 and discovered that "the heavens declare the glory of God," that creation reveals that God is speaking. Continuing on in verses 7–11, we see what David indicates God is actually saying in special revelation:

> *The instruction of the Lord is perfect, renewing one's life; the testimony of the Lord is trustworthy, making the inexperienced wise. The precepts of the Lord are right, making the heart glad; the command of the Lord is radiant, making the eyes light up. The fear of the Lord is pure, enduring forever; the ordinances of the Lord are reliable and altogether righteous. They are more desirable than gold—than an abundance of pure gold; and sweeter than honey, which comes from the honeycomb. In addition, Your servant is warned by them; there is great reward in keeping them.*

Just like any author wants to be interpreted correctly, God expects His people to desire His Word and to properly interpret it by putting into practice all He commands. In Psalm 19:7–11, David reminds us of what we learn in

2 Timothy 3:16–17, namely, that God's special revelation is perfect and trustworthy.

Where Paul tells Timothy that Scripture makes God's children complete and equipped, David sums it up by saying that Scripture makes God's children wise. We do not worship the deist's god, who leaves clues about himself scattered about the universe but then goes hands-off and leaves us to our own deductive devices. No, we worship the God who interrupts us when we're trying to mind our own business, and He tells us His name, His plan, and His complete set of instructions on what to do with them.

God does not want us to fumble around in the shadows, trying to figure out the meaning of life. He tells us where we stand in relation to Him (sinners deserving wrath), how we got there (through Adam's sin, which we both inherit and embrace), and best of all, how we get out of it into a right standing with Him (through Christ's sacrificial death and glorious resurrection). Thanks be to God that He does not expect us to piece these expectations together solely through the changing of the seasons or the pervasive injustice in the world! He tells us straight out.

But David goes further. He not only speaks of the reality of God's expectations in His declarations, he speaks of the quality of these expectations. God's revelation is good for "renewing one's life" (v. 7), "making the heart glad" (v. 8), and "making the eyes light up." They are "more desirable than gold" and "sweeter than honey" (v. 10).

In what ways can God's instructions make the heart glad? In what ways can God's commandments make our eyes light up?

God Reveals His Plan for Redeeming the World and Bringing Glory to Christ

Many of us are not used to thinking of God's commandments—and Scripture in general—as "sweeter than honey," something that is delicious. Even if we can reckon with the idea of loving God's law, we may have trouble figuring out how not to think of it in the context of a religious duty or a "chore chart" (something followed but not particularly enjoyed in my home!). But the psalms speak of God's children delighting in God's law. How in the world do we get to that perspective?

The way we find God's commands delightful and His instruction tasty like honey is by moving beyond what God requires of us and seeing what He has accomplished Himself. As we learned before, God Himself is the Hero of God's story, and as it pertains to His desire to be known, He Himself bridges the communication gap we are unable to span ourselves. He does this first by speaking into the shadows of general revelation in the special revelation of Scripture. He does this savingly by speaking in the special revelation of Scripture the great announcement of the gospel of Jesus.

The point of special revelation, then, is to reveal the gospel. God's written Word points to Jesus, the Living Word. Don't take my word for it, however. Listen to Jesus Himself:

> He said to them, "How unwise and slow you are to believe in your hearts all that the prophets have spoken! Didn't the Messiah have to suffer these things and enter into His glory?" Then beginning with Moses and all the Prophets, He interpreted for them the things concerning Himself in all the Scriptures. (Luke 24:25–27)

After Jesus was raised from the dead, He caught up with a couple of disciples making a trek to Emmaus. He sidled up alongside them and preached the greatest Christ-centered, expository sermon from the Old Testament ever preached in the history of the world. "The point of all that," Jesus essentially said, pointing to the varied wonders of what we call the Old Testament, "is Me."

As Jesus claimed implicitly and explicitly throughout His earthly ministry that He is the true Messiah long awaited by the people of God, He was asserting Himself as the culmination of human history.

> *Reflecting on Jesus' revelation to His traveling companions in Luke 24:25–27, what might have been some of "the things concerning Himself" that He showed them from the Old Testament?*

Reading Scriptures
with Christ at the Center

We can see the light of Christ in the shadow of the "first gospel" in one of the Bible's earliest stories, when God curses the serpent in Genesis 3:15. Here is a foreshadow of the saving cross of Christ, where simultaneously Jesus' heel was struck in crucifixion and He was victorious over sin and death, crushing the head of evil with His pierced feet.

We see the light of Christ in the shadow of the Old Testament's "last gospel," when Malachi 4 predicts the Day of the Lord. Who brings both wrath and redemption? Who is elsewhere referred to as the sun (Rev. 21:23)? Who is said to arrive on this Day of the Lord (Acts 2:17–24; 1 Thess. 5:1–10)? Who alone can do a supernatural work of reconciliation?

The answer is ever and always Jesus. His footprints are throughout the sand of the Old Testament. And the further light of the New Testament helps us see Him most clearly, from His incarnation to His glorification.

All the stories of the Bible tell the unified story of how God glorifies Himself through the redemption of sinners who are made right with Him through the saving work of His Son, Jesus Christ.

None of this means that the Bible doesn't give us what we call "propositional truth." The Bible is not a story in the same way a novel is a story. It is a story in the sense that throughout all its genres and revelations, the overarching theme or message being communicated is that God saves sinners through the life, death, and resurrection of Jesus Christ.

Knowing the "big story" running through and connecting all the words of the Bible, we can see how we might move from duty to delight. When we receive the illumination of Jesus Christ, our eyes light up with the grace of God found in Him who is the radiance of the Father's glory (Heb. 1:3). When we receive Jesus as the Bread of life, we will taste and see that God is good. And when we are set free from our sins and the curse of the law's demands, we are finally free to obey God with joy and gratitude, delighting in His law rather than buckling under its weight. Psalm 19:11 tells us there is "great reward" in keeping God's commands. We can't do that. But Jesus can and did. And there is great reward in Christ's righteousness for all who will repent of their sin, trust in His work, and thereby receive His goodness credited to their account.

Through His Word, God specifies His intentions for humanity and His expectations of us. We are to respond to God's special revelation by aligning ourselves with God's expressed will.

What part of your life is working counter to God's intentions?

Does God's voice have a presence in your life? Are you instructed, rebuked, and corrected by the Word?

Is it possible to revere the Word and not read it? How might one discipline oneself to spend unhurried time in God's Word?

Day 19

In God We Trust

"In God We Trust." We see these words on American currency. We hear these words in patriotic songs such as "The Star-Spangled Banner." The phrase was adopted as the national motto of the United States of America in 1956.

Trust is a serious matter. America's national motto implies both that we are dependent and that God is trustworthy. But do we really trust God?

In the fall of 2008, the unthinkable happened: the "almighty dollar" (as many have dubbed it) was weakened through a series of economic trends that brought the U.S. economy to the brink of disaster. Ironically, as the value of the dollar shrunk, it became apparent that many people had been trusting in it rather than God. The motto turned out to be mere words with very little truth behind them.

The issue of trust goes to the heart of what it means to be human. As we have seen on previous days, God has revealed Himself through what He has created as well as through His Word. God is not silent. He has spoken to us and recorded His words in the Bible. But are we listening? And when we encounter His Word, do we really trust Him?

The Bible teaches that God spoke into being all that exists. The pinnacle of creation is mankind—made in His own image (Gen. 1:27). Then God proclaimed all that He created to be "very good" (v. 31), thus affirming that all of creation was fulfilling His intended purposes. Because God created by His words and because all that He created was "very good," we know that God's words are the source of all that is good. Therefore, God's words can and must be trusted. Initially, God's image-bearers, Adam and Eve, enjoyed a relationship with God as obedient worshipers trusting His good words. "In God We Trust" would have been an appropriate motto for those early days in the garden of Eden.

Our goal is to believe the trustworthiness of God and His Word so that we might grow in worship and obedience through learning to handle God's Word faithfully, but through the fall we have mishandled His Word and misdirected our worship. Can we really say that we trust, worship, and obey God when we question, belittle, and disobey God's Word?

What do the words "In God We Trust" mean to you? Do those words accurately reflect the way you live? Why or why not?

DAY 20

God's Word Is Trustworthy, but We Twist It

Now the serpent was the most cunning of all the wild animals that the LORD God had made. He said to the woman, "Did God really say, 'You can't eat from any tree in the garden'?" The woman said to the serpent, "We may eat the fruit from the trees in the garden." (Gen. 3:1–2)

 Early in the biblical narrative, we find Adam and Eve facing temptation from a crafty and deceitful serpent in the garden of Eden. Many people have missed the point of this historical encounter by focusing on where the serpent came from, what type of fruit he was offering, and whose fault the whole debacle really was. While those questions may be interesting, they are not ones that God deemed crucial to our fulfilling our purpose of living as worshipers in obedience to His Word.

Whenever we approach Scripture, our primary question should be "What does this text say about God?" This particular passage makes clear that the serpent was among the creatures that God made. We know from Genesis 1–2 that God made everything "good," meaning that everything originally functioned according to His purposes. But this serpent entered the garden in order to disrupt the peace of God's creation. At this point, the Bible does not tell us where the serpent came from or who he is. What we do know is that the serpent is crafty. Theologian D. A. Carson notes that the word *crafty* entails "sneakiness . . . [or] someone who is wise and prudent." Part of the "goodness" God bestowed on the being later identified as Satan (literally, "the accuser") is wisdom or prudence. Carson expands: "The serpent, Satan, was crowned with more prudence than all the other creatures, but in his rebelling the prudence became craftiness; the very same virtue that was such a strength became twisted into a vice."

The serpent displayed his twisted wisdom by subtly attacking God's Word and maligning God's character. The serpent spoke: "Did God really say?" The irony of this scene is heavy. The Bible began with God speaking all things into existence—including the serpent. And now the serpent that was created by the word of God has questioned the authority of the One whose word created him! With this subtle question, he usurped the clearly communicated word of God.

What are some examples of how man has taken things that God made "good" and used them for evil purposes?

What are some virtues that Satan twists into vices?

God's Word Is Trustworthy, but We Question It

 "Did God really say?" the serpent asked. Some people do not obey God's Word because they do not believe it to be God's Word. They reject the Word because they see no authority behind it.

Imagine this scene. A group of schoolchildren are enjoying recess time on the playground. The teacher sits quietly on the bench near the swing set. When it's time to go back to class, she tells one of the students to call the others inside. If the children are having a wonderful time, some of them will question the source of their classmate's message. "Who said we have to go in now?" they ask. "The teacher said so!" comes the reply. "Did the teacher really say we have to leave now? How do we know?" they persist. Their desire to stay on the playground will cause them to question the authority of the messenger.

In a similar manner, the serpent planted a seed of doubt in Eve's mind regarding the source of authority: "Did God really say that?" He knew that if she doubted the source of the command, she would disregard it.

"Did God really say?" the serpent asked. Eve responded rightly: "YES! He did."

In Genesis 2:16–17, God explicitly commanded Adam not to eat of the tree of the knowledge of good and evil.

The serpent's question undermined the holy authority of God and maligned the loving character of God. God's word had not restricted Adam and Eve uncaringly; rather, His command offered amazingly abundant choices. In the garden, the man and woman had endless opportunities for obeying God by eating the fruit from any of the other trees. There was only one solitary possibility for disobedience. But it was at the point of the restriction that the serpent made his crafty attack. Eve's response was at least initially hopeful, for she recognized the serpent's subtle error and corrected him. She also maintained the source of the command as being from God. However, in her correction we learn something about ourselves.

> *What are some reasons people deny the truth that God inspired the Scriptures?*

> *Is it possible that some of us deny God's authorship of Scripture because we do not want Scripture to have authority in our lives?*

DAY 22

God's Word Is True,
but We Change It

The woman said to the serpent, "We may eat the fruit from the trees in the garden. But about the fruit of the tree in the middle of the garden, God said, 'You must not eat it or touch it, or you will die.'" "No! You will not die," the serpent said to the woman. "In fact, God knows that when you eat it your eyes will be opened and you will be like God, knowing good and evil." (Gen. 3:2–5)

As this conversation unfolded, Eve's own doubts emerged in the form of her adding a harsh exaggeration to God's Word: "But about the fruit of the tree in the middle of the garden, God said, 'You must not eat it or touch it, or you will die'" (v. 3). Eve belittled God's Word by adding to it. Her addition to the Word of God misrepresented God as a harsh taskmaster.

Some skeptics belittle God's Word by subtracting from it. The third president of the United States of America, Thomas Jefferson, created his own "Bible." He described the process: "We must reduce our volume to the simple evangelists, select, even from them, the very words only of Jesus . . . I have performed this operation for my own use, by cutting verse by verse out of the printed book, and arranging the matter . . . as diamonds in a dunghill."

Others reduce God's Word by adding to it. Joseph Smith, the founder of Mormonism, added to God's Word by claiming that an angel had given him *The Book of Mormon*.

These are extreme examples, but the error of both is the same as that of Eve. Her posture toward the Wword of God demonstrated her desire for independence. D. A. Carson writes: "A lot of people think that 'sin' is: just breaking a rule. What is at stake here is something deeper, bigger, sadder, uglier, more heinous. It is a revolution. It makes me god and thus de-gods God."

In what ways has our culture's obsession with "being true to ourselves" or "being independent" affected our view of God and His Word?

God's Word Is True,
but We Belittle It

 When Satan can't get us to undermine God's Word through outright unbelief, he will try to get us to undermine it through misplaced trust. That's why Eve began to speak authoritative words herself—words that painted God in a negative light. From the account in Genesis we learn that one of the great dangers we face when handling the Word of God is the temptation to place ourselves in the seat of authority over it.

The encounter between the serpent and Eve continued as the serpent then openly defied God's Word: "No! You will not die," the serpent said to the woman. "In fact, God knows that when you eat it your eyes will be opened and you will be like God, knowing good and evil" (vv. 4–5). Satan has now shown his cards. What started as subtle skepticism has become outright rebellion. Satan has implied that God is a liar.

Furthermore, he has undermined the character of God by leading Adam and Eve to believe that God was withholding goodness from them. Our postmodern infatuation with entertainment and social media highlights our desire to make our own truth claims.

Facebook has the "Like" button. Twitter has a "Retweet" button. Both are geared toward receiving the praise of men through their affirmation of one's fleeting expression—whether truthful or not. Today there is even a site that uses public opinion through voting to settle personal disputes about truth claims. The site boasts, "Have a disagreement with someone? Settle it here!" "Everything's Debatable." "Just upload your 30 second argument and let the viewers decide who's right." Just imagine for a moment how crazy things might be if God's Word came to us with this kind of Web site as its medium! But then again, whenever we allow either personal preference or public opinion to shape our understanding of truth, we are standing in judgment over God in much the same way.

How might both public opinion and personal preference negatively shape your understanding of God and His Word?

In what way is questioning God's Word different from asking questions of God's Word?

Day 24

God's Word Is Authoritative, but We Disobey It

Then the woman saw that the tree was good for food and delightful to look at, and that it was desirable for obtaining wisdom. So she took some of its fruit and ate it; she also gave some to her husband, who was with her, and he ate it. (Gen. 3:6)

 God had spoken very plainly to Adam in Genesis 2:17 regarding this prohibited tree. Often men will begin to play the "blame game"—"It was Eve's fault!" We sec this unfold in Genesis 3:12. Adam blamed Eve, and in some sense he also blamed God: "The woman You gave to be with me . . ." In 1 Timothy 2:14, it seems that Paul affirmed that it was Eve who was deceived. But Paul also said in 1 Corinthians 11:3 that man is the head, or steward, over the woman. God had given the commandment to Adam—before Eve was taken from his side. It was Adam's responsibility to teach and protect Eve. But we find Adam standing nearby—silent and complicit.

The point of this story is not about the type of fruit, as if the fruit juices would poison the minds of Adam and Eve. No, the poison of sin coursed through their veins before the fruit entered their mouths. "It was not the nature of the tree that made it dangerous, the bearer of covenant curse and death, but what it stood for: obedience to the word of God."[2]

We know that the serpent, Adam, and Eve all transgressed God's command. Each of them was guilty of disobeying God's word, as are we. And every time we choose to disobey, we are proclaiming to God that we are wiser than He is. We are "crafty" and we deserve condemnation. What happened in the garden is replayed in our own lives every single day. Often when we are tempted, we wonder, *Did God really say?*

Our answer to that question is illustrative of whom we really trust and whom we really worship. When Adam and Eve questioned, belittled, and disobeyed God's Word, they went from being awe-struck worshipers of God to being brazen idolaters worshiping themselves. Worship is at stake in how we approach the Word of God. How we handle and respond to God's Word will show whom we worship.

> *What are some examples of times in your life when you were forced to answer the question "Did God really say?"*
>
> *How did you respond to the temptation to distrust God?*

---

2. Michael D. Williams, *Far as the Curse Is Found* (Phillipsburg, NJ: P&R Publishing, 2005), 67.

God's Word Is Proven
through Jesus

 There is only one person who lived a life that demonstrated without reservation the truth of this statement: "In God I trust." He too was put to the test like Adam and Eve. God placed Adam into a lush garden with endless possibilities to worship and obey and only one prohibition. God drove Jesus into the wilderness where He had no food, water, or shelter. And there Jesus came face-to-face with that crafty serpent who used the same game plan—to get Jesus to question, belittle, and disobey God's Word.

How did Jesus respond? By affirming His trust in God's Word. By uplifting the true intent of God's Word. By obeying God's Word. There in the wilderness, Jesus succeeded where Adam and Eve had failed. And when Jesus laid down His life as an atoning sacrifice for us on the cross, His perfect worship and obedience were made available to us.

Whom are you trusting in today?
Self? Public opinion? Jesus?

How does the fall into sin affect the mission that
God tasked Adam and Eve with? How does our
sin keep us as Christians from carrying out the
responsibilities God has entrusted to us?

God's Law Is Love

 Imagine that you and your spouse are planning to adopt an infant from an impoverished country. When you arrive at the orphanage, you find a malnourished baby girl. You are troubled to see the conditions your child has been living in, but you are overjoyed to know that this will be her last day there. She's coming home!

Once you get back home, you can see your daughter is having difficulty adjusting to her new surroundings. She's not used to bathing daily. She's unaccustomed to the food you give her. She's a bit fussy because of all the changes. Nevertheless, you bear with her, showing great patience because, after all, she is family now.

Time passes and the baby grows into a little girl. Now your role as a parent gets more challenging. You begin to teach her the rules of your home. You patiently teach her what's best for her and for your family.

But one day, she begins to complain about your rules. "Dad and Mom, you're being mean to me! Why won't you let me do this or that?" This is your baby girl—the same one you rescued from a painful life that would've known little in the way of love. And now she is accusing you of being harsh for expecting obedience to such "strict rules"! What your daughter fails to realize, of course, is that had you not adopted her, she wouldn't be under these love-driven rules.

Instead, she would be under rules made by people who were not family. Or worse yet, she might have been put out on the streets by now with no protective relationships in place. Stephen Lennox describes this scenario in his book *God's Story Revealed*, noting that rules given to such a child convey the truth that they are no longer orphaned but are part of a family.

Think back to your own childhood. What did the rules of your home (or lack of rules) communicate to you about your parents?

If you have children now, how do the rules you set for your house convey something about who you are and what kind of life you desire for your children?

Day 27

God's Law for Life

 We have already looked at how the crafty serpent with twisted wisdom tricked Adam and Eve into disobeying God's word. Man and Woman broke their relationship with the God who had made them in His image.

Though their sin had cosmic consequences, God graciously revealed hope for fallen humanity by promising a Rescuer, the Seed of woman, who alone could fix what they had destroyed. Mankind's sin and its effects quickly spread to every aspect of life. But in Genesis 12, God made a covenant promise to a man named Abraham: through his offspring, all the nations would be blessed. The remainder of Genesis traces his lineage and displays God's power to work through seemingly hopeless circumstances to keep His promises. Abraham's children (known collectively as Israel) settled in Egypt, not the land that was promised to their forefather.

When Exodus picks up the story, we find God's chosen people enslaved by Pharaoh in Egypt. God heard the cries of His people, and He chose a man named Moses to serve as a mediator while God Himself would rescue His people and keep His promise. God was coming to make an orphaned slave into His very own "treasured possession."

Once this rescue took place, God revealed that His people's new identity would involve living under a new standard of conduct. God was about to "lay down the law," revealing to His people crucial distinguishing aspects of His own identity as well as aspects of their new identity as His people.

Like Israel, we have been rescued from the tyranny of Satan and our slavery to sin. God has shown us amazing grace in adopting us into His family. As we look back to the law given to Israel, we will grow in our understanding of who God is and see His loving purpose in giving the law. We will also see how the law should shape our identity and how the law shows us our need for Jesus.

How might this understanding of truth affect the way a person views God's speech in the Bible? How might it affect the way a person lives?

Read Psalm 119. How did the psalmist view the commands of God? In particular, identify some of the results of obedience to God's commands.

Day 28

God Has Set a Moral Standard that Expresses His Character

Then God spoke all these words: "I am the LORD your God, who brought you out of the land of Egypt, out of the place of slavery." (Exod. 20:1–2)

 Have you ever gotten "the silent treatment" from someone? Or have you ever known someone who talks all of the time without saying much at all? The ability to communicate is part of what it means to be made in God's image. We have been given the ability to communicate with God and with one another. Lack of clear communication usually means trouble for a relationship.

In Exodus 20, we see God communicating clearly (through Moses) to all of Israel about His expectations of them. These are not merely the ideas of Moses, these are the words of God, and as such, they carry the authority and importance of their true Author. D. A. Carson notes that "(God) is still being presented as a talking God, not only with the kind of speech that calls the universe into existence (Genesis 1–2) and with the kind of speech that interacts with his image bearers (Genesis 3) . . . but with the kind of speech that commands them."

Everyone lives by some moral standard. In our own postmodern era, many people describe truth as relative or unknowable. But even they are making a truth claim that shapes the way they make moral decisions.

Though the Bible is more than just a book of rules, it does indeed make claims that should shape the lives of those who call themselves "Christian." When it comes to God's people, God does not just leave the issue of right and wrong for us to decide. He has a righteous standard that flows out of who He is. If we are to be in relationship with God, we must come to Him on His terms and not our own.

Israel had to learn this lesson. The Israelites had long been living under the authority of Pharaoh and his idolatrous laws. Their life in Egypt affected the way they thought about their own identity. Egyptian culture influenced the way they lived. For example, the Egyptians upheld Pharaoh as a semi-divine being. His authority over the residents of his kingdom was grounded in his being like a god to them. Pharaoh had long portrayed for Israel an improper understanding of God and a moral standard that ran contrary to God's. As a result, Israel's identity had been heavily influenced by Pharaoh's values. Israel had to "unlearn" certain falsehoods in order to see the world rightly and to live according to God's commands.

Why do many people have a deep aversion to the idea that God would command us to do or not do certain things?

How can we demonstrate that God's moral standard is rooted in love?

Does our identity shape our behavior or does our behavior shape our identity? How do identity and behavior relate?

God's Rules Reflect His Character as a Loving Father

 When we speak about someone's character, we sometimes use the phrase "He's a man of his word" to describe trustworthiness. Sometimes politicians are accused of making "hollow promises," a term that means their words can't be trusted. Words are important because they convey the character of the person speaking them.

God is the Master Communicator. His law reflects His perfect moral character. God never speaks hollow words. Just as you can know what kind of father I am to my children by the words I speak to them, God's words reflect who He is. The rules He gives us reflect His character as a loving Father.

Consider the first words Moses recorded when God spoke the Ten Commandments: "I am the LORD your God" (Gen. 20:2). This is covenant language that carries with it not only a statement of fact but of promise. God has revealed Himself to Moses and now to all Israel as "YHWH," or "I AM." He is the eternal and unchanging God.

Watch what comes next. See how God's name becomes synonymous with what He has done for Israel: "I am the LORD your God, who brought you out of the land of Egypt, out of the place of slavery." Though He is the God of all nations, He established a unique relationship with Israel. He became her Redeemer and Rescuer so that she would be His own possession, a kingdom of priests and a holy people. This is the relationship that forms the foundation for all of the Ten Commandments. It is precisely because He has rescued her and restored relationship with her that He demands moral fidelity from her. Israel's new identity is now tied to God's identity!

Imagine getting married and then, after the ceremony, continuing to live as though you were not married. How foolish! Wedding ceremonies form the basis of a commitment intended to shape and protect an ongoing, intimate relationship. Once married, it is right to have expectations of complete fidelity from your spouse.

In the same way, God did not just deliver Israel from the bondage of Egypt, He delivered them into His own presence! They were saved from slavery for God. God's love is signified not only in His delivering us from the bondage of sin but also in His expectations of fidelity from us. Failure to have those expectations would convey apathy and lack of affection, that we don't really belong to Him.

God's law was a gift to Israel that told them how to live as God's chosen people. Ultimately Israel's obedience would make them a "light to the nations" (Isa. 42:6; 49:6) and a "city . . . on a hill" (Matt. 5:14) so that God's global plan of redemption would advance to all peoples. But even with this view of ultimate redemption in place, the law also teaches us how to relate to God and others.

In what ways does understanding God's intention behind the law help us in our desire to be obedient?

How does this keep us from reducing the law to just rules and regulations?

DAY 30

God's Law Teaches Us How to Relate to God and Others

 If we are going to understand God's purpose in giving the Ten Commandments, then we need to see how they are structured. The first four focus vertically on our relationship to God. The last six focus horizontally on our relationship to others. Jesus may have alluded to this structure when He answered the question in Matthew 22:36–40 regarding which command is most important. Jesus quoted Deuteronomy 6:5, "Love the Lord your God with all your heart, with all your soul, and with all your strength." This summarizes the vertical nature of commandments 1–4.

Then Jesus went on to emphasize Leviticus 19:18: "Love your neighbor as yourself." This summarizes the horizontal nature of commandments 5–10. It seems Jesus was saying that the two orientations, God-ward and man-ward, are tied together.

Read Exodus 20:3–11, noting the vertical dimension of the first four commandments.

Now read Exodus 20:12–17, noting the horizontal relational dimension of commandments 5–10.

Just as the commandments have both a vertical and horizontal orientation, violation of the Ten Commandments has both vertical and horizontal consequences.

Take King David, for example. One evening while his army was off to war without him, he went out on his rooftop and saw a beautiful woman bathing. He wanted her for himself (coveting). He took her and had sex with her (theft and adultery). He lied about it (false testimony). He had her husband killed to cover it up (murder). But in his prayer of confession, he told God, "Against You—You alone—I have sinned and done this evil in Your sight" (Ps. 51:4). In keeping with the structure of the Ten Commandments, David's transgression of commandments 6–10 was rooted in his pride and violation of the spirit of the first four. Break one commandment and it's like a house of cards: they all come tumbling down!

What are some examples we see in society of how breaking one commandment leads to breaking another?

How has disobedience in one area of your life led to disobedience in other areas?

Day 31

God's Law Provides Freedom

 When properly understood, God's law provides freedom within its constraints and boundaries. Look back at Exodus 20:3–17. (Flip back to yesterday to see the verses.) Flip the commandments around and you see the freedom that comes from keeping them. You are free to love and commune with the only God who is really God! You are free to love others above yourself!

Remember the household rules for the adopted child we talked about a few days ago? These rules not only display a new identity for the child, they also grant a tremendous amount of freedom. Possibilities in life are opened up to the child that would have otherwise been unrealized simply because that child is now part of a new family.

We've seen that the law God gave His people revealed His character and His grace. It also revealed His people's inability to live up to His standard of righteousness. It is precisely because the law reveals God's goodness that it also reveals our badness. And as we see our sinfulness, we begin to feel our need for grace.

In what ways do rules in your house actually provide freedom for your family members?

Spend time now praising God for the freedoms that He has provided for you by giving you the law.

63

Day 32

God Asks for
Complete Obedience

The apostle Paul notes in Romans 3:23 that all of humanity has fallen short of God's standard. Even partial obedience equals complete disobedience. James 2:10 says, "For whoever keeps the entire law, yet fails in one point, is guilty of breaking it all."

As we saw in the past few days, obedience to God's Word displays trust in God's character. Conversely, disobedience is always rooted in distrust of God. We don't really believe that His way of living is best for us. Even though we believe certain actions to be wrong, we still do them. What does this tell us about our need for the gospel?

All too often, however, we address this failure by trying harder to change our "actual practice," which results in legalism. If we are to avoid legalism, it is crucial that we view the law through the lens of the gospel. God's purpose for the law was always to lead us to Christ.

In what ways do your stated beliefs and your actual practices contradict one another?

What sins do you try to justify by pointing out the laws you do follow?

The Gospel Provides
the Power for Mission

 God gave explicit standards and demanded obedience in order to show us our need for Christ. In speaking of the law, Jesus said, "Don't assume that I came to destroy the Law or the Prophets. I did not come to destroy but to fulfill" (Matt. 5:17).

Where every other human that has ever lived have failed, Christ succeeded. So then, "What the law could not do since it was limited by the flesh, God did. He condemned sin in the flesh by sending His own Son . . . in order that the law's requirement would be accomplished in us" (Rom. 8:3–4). God's law is rooted in His own character. God is holy, and thus, His law is holy. And God demands holiness through faith that produces obedience, not the other way around. The gospel view of the law is that God provided in Christ all that He demands from us. Our proper response is to believe it and then lean upon Him for our growth in obedience and to trust Him for the power to accomplish the mission He has given us.

Ed Stetzer and Philip Nation write in *Compelled by Love*: "The death of Christ upon the Cross makes it possible for missional believers to live lives of love."

How does the Cross make it possible
for you to "live a life of love"?

God Has Adopted You

 Once upon a time you were living as an orphan, destitute and impoverished with regard to God's righteous standard. But God came to you. He adopted you and gave you a new identity. As He welcomed you into His family, He gave you guidelines to live by.

The purpose of these laws is not to constrain you but rather to set you free to be everything He has created you to be.

Some people view God's law as limiting rather than liberating, but within the Bible's story line, we can see the law as a description of a life of joyous freedom under the God who has made us. The law reveals our need for salvation but is powerless to save us. The gospel message is that even as God legislates, He points us to Jesus, who has kept the law in our place, thereby making our obedience possible.

Consider the reasons for God's gift of the law. What does obeying God have to do with our mission as Christ's followers?

How can we emphasize obedience in a way that makes clear the need for heartfelt, inside-out transformation and not merely legalism?

Day 35

Numb to the Word

 "Unclean! Unclean!" The shout resounded through the narrow streets of Palestine. Jewish ceremonial law rendered anyone with leprosy to be unclean. Any physical contact with lepers (even their shadow) would make you ceremonially unclean and exclude you from worship activities.

Why were lepers treated with such disdain? One reason concerned the disfigurement caused by the skin disease. A face without a nose is a scary sight. Fingers, toes, and other extremities were often missing. That's why anyone who had this infectious disease was considered an "outcast" by the rest of society. "Colonies" of lepers formed in order to provide social interaction for this ragged bunch of outcasts.

Leprosy is a disease that adversely affects the nervous system. It gradually numbs a person's extremities to the point that pain is no longer felt.

You might think that never feeling pain would be a good thing, right? After all, if you're going to get a filling in a tooth, you're thankful for that shot of Novocain! And if you're going to have surgery, you schedule an anesthesiologist. Pain is bad, right? In the case of a cavity or a cut, we want to avoid needless pain. But what if the numbing from the Novocain was permanent? What if the sensation of pain never returned to your mouth? Over time, you'd chew your tongue off!

Pain serves a purpose. In fact, it is a gift from God and part of His creation order. Pain tells a child not to touch a hot stove. Pain tells a carpenter to aim skillfully with a hammer. Pain warns and guides. And that's the problem with leprosy. Lepers are numb to pain, which means they don't know when their hand is burning or when they've just hit their thumb with a hammer. Lepers literally destroy their own bodies through their actions. Why? Because they can't feel anything. They don't sense that anything is wrong until it's too late.

But there's more to "feeling" than just pain. What about feeling good things? A leper doesn't feel pain. But neither can lepers feel the gentle touch of someone who cares for them. Numbness eliminates all feelings—the painful feelings given to protect you and the good feelings given to bless and encourage you. The numbness of leprosy results in "death by a thousand cuts." What a horrible disease! More horrible than physical leprosy is spiritual numbness—the inability to recognize our sin and how it harms us and the inability to recognize God's grace and how it benefits us. Sin sears our consciences, leading us away from life—in all its beauty and complexity. The end result is spiritual death.

Have you ever felt numb to God's Word?

What attitudes or decisions lead to spiritual numbness? How does a person begin to "feel" again?

Day 36

What Happens When
You Are Numb

 In Exodus 20, God spoke to the Israelites in order to show them how they should relate to Him vertically and how they should relate to one another horizontally.

Unfortunately, the remainder of the Old Testament painstakingly documents Israel's indifference to God's gracious Word. Where once it was Pharaoh who hardened his heart upon hearing the word of the Lord delivered through Moses, now the very people whom God had rescued chose to suppress the truth of God's Word. Israel's history is marked by cycles of disobedience, judgment, and deliverance.

The irony is that Israel's hearts proved to be much harder than the stone tablets upon which God had written His commands. But God promised through Jeremiah, "I will put My teaching within them and write it on their hearts. I will be their God, and they will be My people" (31:33). Spiritual leprosy would not have the last word!

The Bible teaches that we have long suffered from spiritual leprosy ever since human beings sinned.

*Pray for God to bring feeling to your heart
and show you the areas of your life where you
are burning yourself without realizing.*

Day 37

We Suppress the Truth

And you were dead in your trespasses and sins in which you previously walked according to the ways of this world, according to the ruler who exercises authority over the lower heavens, the spirit now working in the disobedient. (Eph. 2:1–2)

For the wages of sin is death, but the gift of God is eternal life in Christ Jesus our Lord. (Rom. 6:23)

In Ephesians 2:1–2, we learn that apart from Christ we are spiritually dead. What does it look like for us to be dead in our trespasses and sins and to walk according to the ways of this world? The apostle Paul shines further light on this "spiritual deadness" in Romans 1–2. There he shows that we suppress the truth made available to us in general revelation (through creation) and also the truth made available to us in special revelation (God's direct Word to us).

So first, we suppress the truth of general revelation. This suppression comes out in several ways. For example, the pantheist declares that all of nature is God. The deist declares that God has nothing to do with the day-to-day workings of nature. Some people are so consumed with the creation that they fail to honor the Creator. Each of these positions is wrong, and they lead us to a warped view of creation and the Creator.

In His goodness, God has shown Himself to us in creation. But rather than glorify God or show gratitude, mankind has suppressed and disobeyed this God-speech and turned to idolatry. Our acts of suppression, disobedience, and idolatry always lead to death because they cut us off from the One through whom all life exists.

Second, we suppress the truth of special revelation, meaning we disregard God's direct Word to us. Paul often spoke of his own people as resting in their identity as God's chosen, in their possession of the law, in God's ownership of them, and in the ability to know His will. The tragedy was that God's people had abused these gifts and disobeyed God's law. If the Gentiles were guilty for suppressing their general knowledge of God, how much more the Jews for their outright disobedience of their special knowledge of God! What's worse, Jewish hypocrisy had resulted in God Himself being blasphemed.

In what ways does the church's hypocrisy reflect a suppression of God's Word?

What sins have we in the church made "respectable"?

What has been the response of the lost world around us?

Disobedience Cuts Us Off

 Disobedience results in death. We exchange life for death. We rebel against God as our Master only to find we are now enslaved by another master—the Evil One. And our spiritual deadness leads to more and more sin.

Our suppression of God's revelation shows that we don't value God's Word as we should. Because we don't recognize the value of God and His Word, we exchange the truth of God for a lie. We have become comfortable trading in counterfeit currency—so comfortable that we are unable to recognize the voice of God apart from His gracious intervention.

If God's standard is perfect righteousness (and it is) and we are filled with all unrighteousness (and we are), then God's Word says that we deserve death. In Romans 6:23, Paul speaks of the wages earned by the sinner as being "death"—not just physical death, though that is certainly on the horizon. The death that Paul speaks of is the same death that God warned Adam about in Genesis 2:17. This is worse than physical death, which separates us from God's world. Paul is speaking here also of spiritual death, which separates us eternally from God Himself. Sin earns death.

What are some lies that our world believes in contrast

to the truth of God revealed through creation?

Day 39

Our Best Efforts to Fix Ourselves Are in Vain

All of us have become like something unclean, and all our righteous acts are like a polluted garment; all of us wither like a leaf, and our iniquities carry us away like the wind. (Isa. 64:6)

 In the spring of 2011, Oprah Winfrey ended her long-running daily television show by hosting a variety of guests and celebrating the shows success. In the final few minutes, she took the stage much like a preacher. And the sermon to her adoring fans was about the root of our pain and suffering. She said: "There is a common thread that runs through all of our pain and all of our suffering, and that is unworthiness. Not feeling worthy enough to own the life you were created for. Even people who believe they deserve to be happy and have nice things often don't feel worthy once they have them." She went on to tell the audience: "Your being alive makes worthiness your birthright. You alone are enough." Oprah's counsel to her massive television audience stands in direct contradiction to the Bible's view of our problem. Scripture doesn't teach us merely that we feel unworthy but that we are unworthy. And when we trace the signs of our brokenness and pain, we find the root cause of sin, and at the bottom of sin is unbelief.

All sin is rooted in unbelief. Each time we knowingly (or unknowingly) transgress God's righteous standard, we are doing so because we believe something (or someone) more than we believe God. The Greek word for *sin* carries the connotation of "missing the mark," as an archer might miss the bulls-eye on a target. The biblical authors go even further: We're not just missing the target, we are aimed in the opposite direction!

We're not just making mistakes. We are all filled with all unrighteousness, so that even the good things we do are tainted by unrighteous motives. No amount of cheerleading our own "worthiness" will make us truly worthy of God's love.

*In what ways is sin related to unbelief
in the promises of God?*

*Why might we prefer the word "mistakes" over "sin"
when speaking of our attitudes and actions?*

Day 40

Our Best Efforts to Fix Ourselves Are for Vanity

 In Genesis 3, we read that after Adam and Eve sinned, they immediately made coverings for themselves in the form of fig leaves. This was a vain attempt to fix themselves. Why did they feel the need to cover their nakedness when just moments before, in Genesis 2:25, they "were naked, yet felt no shame"? The implicit reasoning is that once they suppressed the truth of God ("you will certainly die") and believed the lie of the serpent ("you will not die"), their eyes were opened and they now felt guilt and shame.

The feeling of guilt is a gift from God, much like nerve endings are to the human body. Guilt helps us avoid those things that are destructive in our lives. It is an internal working of the Spirit prompting the conscience when we abandon the righteous standard of God. Shame is the emotional or physical response to guilt. When improperly handled, guilt and shame drive us deeper into sin by causing us to hide in the bushes, much like Adam and Eve.

When the first man and woman covered themselves with fig leaves, it was because they recognized that they no longer met God's righteous standard. Fig leaves wither, thus making their efforts in vain. Had God not graciously replaced the leaves with skins, Adam and Eve would have been forced to cover themselves over and over in one act of vanity after another.

Isaiah 64 makes it clear that no one will be saved because of personal effort. Paul says the same in Romans 3:20: "For no one will be justified in His sight by the works of the law, because the knowledge of sin comes through the law.

When we discussed the role of the law and our response, it was clear that God didn't give us the law as a means to get right with Him through our effort. He gave the law to make us realize that we are broken and can't fix ourselves. Every time we transgress the law, if the Spirit of God is working in us, we feel that merciful twinge of guilt. Like a hot stove screams at your fingertips, "Move or my heat will destroy you!" the law of God shouts at transgressors like you and me: "You're not able! Run to Jesus!"

*Is it possible to run from God while
trying to earn His favor?*

*How can our "best efforts" get in
the way of true salvation?*

*How does our inability to save ourselves provide
a platform for God to display His glory?*

DAY 41

Our Best Desires Are Insufficient for Salvation

As it is written: There is no one righteous, not even one. There is no one who understands; there is no one who seeks God. All have turned away; all alike have become useless. There is no one who does what is good, not even one. (Rom. 3:10–12)

 When I was fourteen, I had a moment. I started to see that the way I was living did not line up with the stories that I heard in Sunday school. So I did what many people who are brought up in the Bible Belt do. I waited until the end of the worship service on a particular Sunday morning and went to the front. When our elderly pastor stepped down to greet me, I told him, "I want to straighten my life up."

Unfortunately, my pastor replied by saying, "Okay. You're going to get baptized." I left church that morning on cloud nine. I was ready to change! By evening, I had fallen from cloud nine without a parachute! But I went ahead and got baptized anyway, hoping that it would do some good. No change. Despite my best desires, I wasn't able to "straighten my life up." My best desires wouldn't save me.

In Romans 3, Paul quotes a number of Old Testament texts to drive home the point that "there is no one righteous

. . . there is no one who seeks God" (Pss. 14:1–3; 53:1–3; Eccl. 7:20; Pss. 5:9; 10:7; 140:3; Isa. 59:7–8; Ps. 36:1).

None of us really pursues God on our own. But what about that neighbor who has been asking questions about church? What about those years that I listened to sermons and felt guilty? Are these not examples of seeking God? Yes and no. Yes, many people show interest in God long before their conversion. But no, that interest is not their doing. The bottom line is this: If a person is seeking God, it is because the Spirit is at work.

What are some signs in a person's life that indicate God's work in preparing their heart for salvation?

How can we discern these signs in order to share the gospel?

DAY 42

Our Best Desires Are Insufficient to Change Us

 In Genesis 1–2, God created man and woman in His own image, and the result was nothing short of glorious. "Glory" carries the connotation of "weightiness." There was a glory to the man and woman in relation to the rest of creation because they reflected God's own glory. They had the distinct privilege of being God's stewards over all that He had created as they lived in perfect harmony with God. But then the man and woman fell from that glory. Their ability to accurately reflect God's glory was lost. They were still in His image, but that image was fractured. All creation suffered as a result. Mankind had "fallen short of the glory of God."

In the Old Testament, the people of Israel waited each year for the Day of Atonement for the assurance that their sins were forgiven. On that day, the high priest would take a blood sacrifice into the tent of meeting where God's presence dwelled, and he would sprinkle the blood on a place called the mercy seat in the holy of holies, where the glory of God rested. They had one chance. Everything was riding on one man to get the job done. But entering into the presence of God was terrifying because God's standard was perfect righteousness and nobody had it.

So take my personal scenario from yesterday. Look back if you do not remember it. For me to "straighten my life up," I would have had to march right in there myself— and I would've fallen short of God's glory! According to the Scriptures, I would have dropped dead on the spot. Why? Even my best intentions to change are tainted with sin. On my best days, I still fail to live up to God's righteous standard. How could I enter into God's presence on my own when I was aimed in the wrong direction? I was indeed lost.

Thankfully, by the grace of God, my heart was not too hardened to hear from God. The Holy Spirit drew me into an authentic relationship with Christ when I was twenty-one. I had grown numb, but Jesus stretched out His hand and touched me. Immediately, I was cleansed (Matt. 8:3).

When is a time that you tried to change
in your own power? Did it work?

What areas of your life have you seen God change?

DAY 43

Are You Ignoring God?

 Humans were created to relate to God and one another. God has spoken clearly telling us how to live, but all too often, we ignore Him. We plug our ears and continue in the path of Frank Sinatra as if "doing it my way" works. All the while, God's Spirit convicts and prompts, beckoning us to repentance so that we may live. After a while, our hearts are so hard and calloused that they no longer feel conviction. We've become spiritual lepers! Like those in Jesus' day, lepers have a tendency of gathering together in shared misery.

The gospel says that Jesus still touches lepers—and when He does, feeling is restored. What was once disfigured and dead is made whole and alive! When we repent and turn to Christ at the sound of His voice, numbness flees and we are enabled to feel the pleasure of His love evermore in His presence. You need no longer bear the internal pain of being "unclean." You have been made clean and now are free to gather with others who have been made clean in a new colony called the "church"—the people tasked with spreading the message of hope to a world of spiritual lepers.

Charles Spurgeon famously said that evangelism is nothing more than one beggar telling another beggar where to find bread. Applying Spurgeon's insight to leprosy, we might say God's mission goes forth when His people, whom He has healed of spiritual leprosy, go out and tell other spiritual lepers about the Savior who is willing to stretch out His hand and heal them too.

The church is a colony of former lepers. It's not a club for people who are perfect but an assembly of people who through God's grace have been forgiven and cleansed and whose lives are looking more and more like the Savior who healed them. We are no longer spiritual lepers whose lives are marked by uncleanness. Instead, the good news of Christ's healing power must resound from our lips and be demonstrated in our lives.

Are you more sensitive to God's Word and voice now than when you first believed?

How does our being healed of spiritual leprosy lead us to take the message of healing to the spiritual lepers around us?

Jesus: The Faithful Son Who Obeys God's Word

 Across countries and cultures, people from all walks of life sense deep down that this life is not all there is. If you were to poll your family and friends, you would find that regardless of their ethnicity or culture, most of them harbor a hope for a life beyond this one, a life of eternal peace and joy.

The "holy books" of other religions have offered ways by which a follower may enter into the next life. Islam, for example, teaches that if you follow the Five Pillars, you will enter paradise. Buddhism offers an eightfold path to nirvana (freedom from suffering). Regardless of the religion, the answer is the same: you must do something to become acceptable in order to enter the next world.

The problem with the solutions provided by other religions is that you can never know if you've done enough to become acceptable to enter the next life. Tim Keller writes: "Self-salvation through good works may produce a great deal of moral behavior in your life, but inside you are filled with self-righteousness, cruelty, and bigotry, and you are miserable. You are always comparing yourself to other people, and you are never sure you are being good enough. You cannot, therefore, deal with your hideousness and self-absorption through the moral law, by trying to be a good person through an act of the will. You need a complete transformation of the very motives of your heart."[3]

The gospel provides what the various religions of the world cannot—the kind of assurance of eternal life that transforms our hearts and lives. You see, every person in the world, including you and me, must face the question "What will it take to be acceptable to enter into eternal life?" The religions say there is work we must do. The gospel takes us back to a work that has been done.

Spend some time in prayer thanking God that the work has been completed and that there is nothing we add or take away from what Jesus has done.

3. Tim Keller, *The Reason for God* (New York, NY: Penguin Books, 2009),177

Day 45

Our Way to Acceptance

When all the people were baptized, Jesus also was baptized. As He was praying, heaven opened, and the Holy Spirit descended on Him in a physical appearance like a dove. And a voice came from heaven: "You are My beloved Son. I take delight in You!" (Luke 3:21–22)

 We all want to be accepted. Think about it—whether it's acceptance and affirmation from our parents, peers at school, coworkers, or even strangers, we all want to be accepted and affirmed. Why do you think we take so much time in making sure we look a certain way (fashion), talk a certain way (lingo, jargon), and behave a certain way (cultural etiquette)?

The desire to be accepted by others is a distortion of the desire God has placed in each of us to be accepted and affirmed by Him. The ultimate acceptance and affirmation we need comes from God. We know deep in our bones that something is wrong with us. The Bible confirms that feeling of uneasiness, informing us that we are not acceptable to God because of our sin.

Though many sincere people follow the teachings of various religions in order to be accepted by God, the Bible tells us that our sin makes us unacceptable. One of the

Scripture passages from last week's lesson told us our best efforts to attain righteousness are in vain (see Isa. 64:6).

*Are you motivated by others'
acceptance and affirmation?*

*What are some ways people seek
affirmation from others?*

*If even our best deeds are in vain, is there any
hope of being accepted and affirmed by God?*

*How do people try to overcome the fear of
not measuring up to God's standard? To
the standard of people around them?*

God the Father Affirms that Jesus Is Uniquely Qualified

 God has spoken to us in His Word and through creation. We have rejected His Word and chosen to go our own way. We need God to fix what we broke in order that we might be reconciled to Him. The Bible gives us good news. We do not have to fear being rejected by God because God Himself has provided a way by which sinners may be accepted before Him. Luke, the evangelist, records the baptism of Jesus of Nazareth in order to show us that Jesus was uniquely qualified to provide the way for sinners to be accepted before God.

First, Jesus was uniquely qualified to bring us to God because He was the Lord's anointed, the Messiah-Christ. God had previously promised He would send a Servant who would carry our sorrows and bear our sins (Isa. 53:4–6). The Coming One would be anointed by the Holy Spirit to accomplish God's mission to seek and save the lost. Luke identifies Jesus as the promised Anointed One (Christ) who came to liberate God's people from sin's slavery (Luke 4:16–21; see Isa. 61:1–2).

Second, Jesus was uniquely qualified to bring us to God because He was and is God's faithful Son, and the Father is pleased with His obedience (Luke 3:22). Jesus is the faithful and obedient Son who was empowered by the Holy Spirit to save God's people by fulfilling the righteousness God required in order to bring them to God. Though Jesus had never sinned, He identified with His sinful people by being baptized.

Here we see the distinction between religion and the gospel. Religion is about what you must do in order to be accepted before God; Christianity is about what God has done for you in order to accept you. As Tim Keller has said, "In religion, we try to obey the divine standards out of fear. We believe that if we don't obey we are going to lose God's blessing in this world and the next. In the gospel, the motivation is one of gratitude for the blessing we have already received because of Christ."[4] This is the good news of the gospel—through faith in Christ, the Lord's anointed, we can be accepted before a holy God. And those whom God accepts He also empowers by His Holy Spirit for obedience and ministry!

Do you struggle with believing the Father has accepted you in Christ?

How does understanding the message of Christianity (the gospel) liberate people from bondage to sin?

4. Ibid., 180.

Day 47

Jesus Obeys Where We Stray

Then Jesus returned from the Jordan, full of the Holy Spirit, and was led by the Spirit in the wilderness for 40 days to be tempted by the Devil. He ate nothing during those days, and when they were over, He was hungry. The Devil said to Him, "If You are the Son of God, tell this stone to become bread." But Jesus answered him, "It is written: Man must not live on bread alone. (Luke 4:1–4)

 When we think of a substitute, our minds likely take us back to school where the substitute teacher was never as good as the "real thing." School kids tend to treat the substitute teacher with disrespect. After all, substitutes have little authority because they have no part in establishing the lesson plan and exercising control over the students' grades. Our experience of a classroom substitute is quite different than the Bible's presentation of Jesus as a substitute for sinful humanity. We think of a substitute as a temporary and poor replacement for the "real thing," but the Bible presents those who came before Jesus as the copies, or types, who pointed to Jesus, who is the real thing. Let's go back to the beginning and look at Adam as an example. Adam, the first man, represented us before God. God spoke His word to Adam, letting him know how to live as God's obedient son (Gen. 2:15–17).

Unfortunately, Adam failed; he and Eve listened as the serpent questioned and distorted God's Word, leading them to disobedience (3:1–8). Since he was our representative, when Adam sinned against God, we sinned with him, which made us guilty and unacceptable before a holy God (Rom. 5:12, 18–19).

In our individualist society, it is difficult for people to understand how one person's sin can affect other people. Why is it important that we maintain the biblical teaching that Adam's sin is passed down to us?

Even today, Satan is still up to his old tricks of distorting God's Word and deceiving us into thinking it says something other than what God has spoken. Consider the tragic incident of racism and slavery in American history. Professing Christians defended slavery on the basis that Africans were less than human. On those grounds, certain Christian theologians defended slavery, even claiming it would help evangelize the heathens!

Can you think of other examples when God's Word has been misused to justify sin?

Have you ever been confused about God's Word and what God desires of us?

How did the Holy Spirit correct your false thinking?

DAY 48

Jesus Obeys God at
the Very Point We Failed

The nation of Israel was also God's representative people, the descendants of Abraham through whom God would bless the world (Gen. 12:1–3). God made a promise to His people: "Now if you will listen to Me and carefully keep My covenant, you will be My own possession out of all the peoples, although all the earth is Mine, and you will be My kingdom of priests and My holy nation" (Ex. 19:5–6).

As God's treasured, firstborn son (4:22), Israel was to serve as God's priests, declaring God's name to the nations so that the world would know He alone is God. Yet just like Adam, Israel failed to obey God's Word. So God made them wander in the wilderness for forty years (Num. 14:33–34). The Gospels shine a spotlight on Jesus, the Messiah of Israel. He was the true representative and substitute for sinful humanity. Jesus faced the Devil as Adam did, and Jesus fought temptation in the wilderness, just like Israel. But unlike Adam and Israel, Jesus succeeded in the mission. He obeyed God at every point they failed. Jesus is the faithful Adam and the faithful Israel who obeyed God's Word.

Jesus responded to Satan's temptations by quoting Deuteronomy 8:3; 6:13, 16. In these passages, Israel was preparing to cross the Jordan River and enter the promised land. By quoting from Deuteronomy, Jesus identified

Himself with Israel. In other words, whereas Israel failed to obey God's Word as they prepared to cross the Jordan River, Jesus kept God's Word after crossing through the waters of baptism and fighting temptation—by trusting (and quoting!) the very word God had given to Israel.

Jesus is a faithful representative and substitute because He fulfilled all righteousness. He was obedient to God's Word at the exact point where Adam and Israel failed. That means Jesus is our faithful representative and substitute too. He has fulfilled all righteousness by being obedient to the Father where you and I have failed.

This is the good news of the gospel. The Father accepts Jesus' obedience on behalf of those who put their trust in Christ. We are unacceptable before a holy God, but Jesus is acceptable, and God affirms Jesus because He pleased the Father (Luke 3:22). By faith in Jesus Christ, we are acceptable to God and receive the same affirmation. The words the Father uttered over Jesus at His baptism ("You are My beloved Son. I take delight in You!") are true of us as well.

When you trust Jesus for your acceptance before a holy God, you are liberated from sin's slavery and curse. After all, this is what Jesus came to do—to restore what sin has destroyed.

What Old Testament book did Jesus quote from?

What is the context of the verses Jesus quoted, and what do you think His quotes indicated for people in His day?

What does that teach us about fighting sin and temptation?

Day 49

Jesus' Obedience to God's Word Proves His Authority

When the sun was setting, all those who had anyone sick with various diseases brought them to Him. As He laid His hands on each one of them, He would heal them. Also, demons were coming out of many, shouting and saying, "You are the Son of God!" But He rebuked them and would not allow them to speak, because they knew He was the Messiah. (Luke 4:40–41)

 Because of sin, God's good creation has been infiltrated by all kinds of evil: disease, death, chaos, and poverty. Sin has tarnished God's good creation, leaving its awful effects all around us, including in our own bodies that waste away due to age and disease. The Bible goes so far as to say that we are enslaved to sin and its effects (Rom. 6:17–22).

As God's Messiah, Jesus not only fulfilled all righteousness by identifying with humanity and obeying where we've failed, but He also announced the good news of God's kingdom (Luke 4:42–44). Jesus' arrival marked the beginning of the kingdom of God, the rule of God where the effects of sin on creation were to be halted and reversed and God's people were to be liberated from sin's hold on them.

Since Jesus was the Messiah, anointed by God's Spirit to accomplish God's mission, Jesus had authority over all creation (5:1–10; 8:22–25). Jesus displayed this authority when He liberated people from physical bondage by healing their diseases (4:38–40) and from spiritual bondage by casting out their demons (vv. 41–44). B. B. Warfield, the famous Princeton theologian, described Christ's work this way: "When our Lord came down to earth He drew heaven with Him. The signs which accompanied His ministry were but the trailing clouds of glory which He brought from heaven, which is His home. The number of the miracles which He wrought may easily be underrated. It has been said that in effect He banished disease and death from Palestine for the three years of His ministry."

To what do unbelieving people attribute all the evil, chaos, and disorder in our world?

What does the Bible say is the source of the evil in our world?

What do unbelievers think will put an end to the chaos and evil around us?

What does the Bible say will put an end to the chaos and evil around us?

DAY 50

The Already/Not Yet Nature of God's Kingdom

Jesus' healings and exorcisms were not only proof of His authority as God's Messiah, they were also a foretaste of the future arrival of God's kingdom in its fullness when there would be no more disease and no more evil. The fact that we still experience sickness and evil today, including demon possession, indicates that though Jesus inaugurated the kingdom of God at His first coming, it has not fully arrived. Though there is a sense that in Jesus the kingdom is already here, until Jesus comes again, the kingdom will not yet fully arrive. Only when Jesus returns will there be no more pain, sorrow, disease, death, chaos, or evil (Rev. 21:1–4).

Ed Stetzer uses a popular illustration to describe the "already" and "not yet" nature of God's kingdom. "As World War II came to a close, there were two important dates. The first one occurred on June 6th, 1944. History remembers it as 'D-day.' As a part of Operation Overlord, the United States and its allies landed on the beach of Normandy, France. It was the beginning of the end of the war. Yet the war in Europe didn't end until more than a year later on May 7, 1945, also known as 'VE-day.'

Despite the fact that the victory at Normandy effectively broke the back of the Axis powers, the war didn't officially end until months later. In fact, more people died in between those dates than any other period of the war. It was dark and difficult, but the end had begun. It was inaugurated June 6, 1944, but the end wasn't consummated until May 7, 1945. That's the difference between D-day and VE-day.

That's not a perfect parallel, but when the kingdom of God arrived in the person of Jesus, it came near. But, it will not be fully realized until Jesus returns at the end of time. The church is left to live between the times."[5] Until the day of Christ's return, those who have put their trust in Jesus Christ and have stopped trusting in their own works for acceptance before God live with the confident hope that we are accepted before God because of Jesus' righteousness. Even though we may still fail to obey and fall into sin, we receive God's forgiveness granted to us through Christ's obedience to God's Word.

As we await the return of Christ, the Father is placing every enemy under Jesus' feet (Eph. 1:22). After Jesus has defeated all His enemies, including death, He will deliver the kingdom to the Father, and we will enter into God's final rest, where we will finally be free from sin and disease and death (1 Cor. 15:24–28).

How does a future hope of being in God's presence where there is no sin, suffering, sorrow, and death help you face sin, suffering, sorrow, and death now?

How does a future hope of no sickness or suffering influence our mission as Christ's representatives in the world?

5. Ed Stetzer, *Subversive Kingdom* (Nashville, TN: LifeWay Press, 2011), 27.

Day 51

Jesus

 Jesus fulfilled the righteousness God requires of humanity by identifying with God's previous sinful human representatives (Adam and Israel) and reenacting their lives at the very points they failed. Christ's obedience began to reverse the effects of sin unleashed upon God's people and the created world. Jesus was uniquely qualified to fulfill God's mission because He was the Lord's anointed, the Messiah-Christ.

As those who are accepted by God through Christ, we too have been empowered by the Holy Spirit for mission and ministry. The Bible declares that we are "a chosen race, a royal priesthood, a holy nation, a people for His possession" (1 Pet. 2:9). In other words, though in and of ourselves we are unacceptable to God, in Christ we are not only acceptable to God but God affirms us, calling us His sons and daughters and sending us out to accomplish His mission—to "proclaim the praises of the One who called you out of darkness into His marvelous light."

Now Jesus is working through us, in the power of the Holy Spirit, to continue telling the world that He alone is God and the only pathway to the Father. As we proclaim this good news of God's kingdom, we will see people liberated from bondage to sin.

If you believe that you are accepted by God through Christ and that God has affirmed you as His child because of Christ and has set you apart to accomplish His mission in the power of the Holy Spirit, then are you being obedient as God's child in fulfilling God's mission?

What are some ways you can join God's mission to proclaim freedom to those who are under sin's curse?

Prayer of Response

"Teach us how to fight by faith against the power of sin, in the confidence that Christ has purchased our forgiveness and secured the triumph of all who trust in him. Turn every evil design of the devil into sanctifying schemes of love. Deliver us from his deceptions. Keep the beauty of Christ clear in the eyes of our heart. Make us instruments of Satan's defeat until you come and slay him by the breath of your mouth. Make us valiant in delivering others by the sword of the Spirit, the Word of God, your great gospel. In Jesus' name we pray, amen."[6] —John Piper

---

6. John Piper, *Seeing and Savoring Jesus Christ* (Wheaton, IL: Crossway, 2004), 80

Jesus: The Faithful Teacher

 Do you find the Old Testament hard to understand (and sometimes hard to believe)? Are there parts of the Old Testament that make you cringe? If so, you're not alone. A good number of people today openly question the validity and value of the Old Testament. Some even go so far as to question the reality of the Old Testament God.

In his book *The God Delusion*, evolutionary biologist Richard Dawkins emphatically states: "The God of the Old Testament is arguably the most unpleasant character in all fiction: jealous and proud of it; a petty, unjust, unforgiving control-freak; a vindictive, bloodthirsty ethnic cleanser; a misogynistic, homophobic, racist, infanticidal, genocidal, filicidal, pestilential, megalomaniacal, sadomasochistic, capriciously malevolent bully." Talk about a litany of negative characteristics! (In case you couldn't tell from reading this quote, Dawkins is an avowed atheist.)

Throughout church history, there have been those who have registered their distaste for the Old Testament and the law-giving God portrayed there. The most famous was Marcion, son of the bishop of Sinope in Pontus around AD 144. Marcion believed that Jesus' teaching contradicted the Old Testament. In his view, the Old Testament God (Yahweh) was vindictive and evil, while the New Testament God (the Father) was loving and gracious in sending Jesus into the world as Savior. So Marcion rejected the Old Testament and proposed a list of books that should be considered as authoritative for the church. His list included only those New Testament books that allowed him to maintain his pitting of Jesus against the Old Testament. (In the end, all he was left with was a mangled version of Luke's Gospel and a handful of chopped up letters from Paul.) Christians rightly rejected the views of Marcion. Even today, we recoil at Marcion's teachings. But even if we would never think of ourselves as modern-day Marcionites, might it be possible that our approach to the Old Testament sometimes resembles Marcion's in practice? Let's consider some diagnostic questions:

- Do we value the Old Testament?
- Do we read and meditate on it?
- Do we seek to apply it to our lives?
- Do we gravitate primarily (or even solely) to the New Testament in our Bible reading and study?
- Do we reduce the Old Testament to little more than illustrative material for the New?

These questions can help us discern a faulty view of the Old Testament. Why does this matter? Because, as the quote from Richard Dawkins illustrates so well, one's view of the Bible and one's view of God go hand in hand.

What negative images of the God of the Old Testament do you or the people around you have?

How might negative views of God affect a person's desire to read and study the Old Testament?

Jesus Fulfilled the Law by Rightly Interpreting It

"Don't assume that I came to destroy the Law or the Prophets. I did not come to destroy but to fulfill."
(Matt. 5:17)

 It's not difficult to see why someone might assume that Jesus came to destroy the Old Testament. After all, Jesus taught that His coming signified a new era, one that marked the end of certain Old Testament commands and institutions, such as food laws (Mark 7:19), the temple (Matt. 24:1–2), and the entire sacrificial system (Heb. 8:13; 10:1–18).

Think of some stories when Jesus acted in a way that challenged the prevailing understanding of the law in His day (see Matt. 9:1–8, 14–15; 12:1–13). Contrary to the assumption that Jesus came to destroy the Old Testament, Jesus declared that His teaching was in complete harmony with it—all of it. In fact, Jesus said that not even the smallest, seemingly inconsequential parts of the words of the law would pass away "until all things are accomplished" (Matt. 5:18).

The Law and the Prophets pointed to a future time when all of its commands, promises, and institutions would be fulfilled. With Jesus' coming, the time of fulfillment had arrived. That is why Jesus explained His mission in relation to the Old Testament—"I [came] . . . to fulfill" (v. 17).

Jesus fulfilled the Law and the Prophets because they pointed to Him. The right way to interpret the Old Testament is by following Jesus' lead in seeing how it is all about Him! Jesus is the true and faithful Israel whom God called out of Egypt (2:15) and who did not put the Lord to the test during His wilderness wandering (4:1–11). Jesus is the new temple who fulfills the old one that was destroyed (John 2:18–22). Jesus is the real bread from heaven (manna) that gives life to the world (6:30–35). Jesus is "the Lamb of God, who takes away the sin of the world" (1:29).

With unique authority, Jesus taught that we cannot understand the Old Testament apart from Him; He is the interpretive lens through which we must understand the Hebrew Scriptures. This means that Jesus was faithful to teach God's Word precisely because He explained God's Word in light of Himself. Only Jesus could provide the faithful and true interpretation of God's Word.

What are some other Old Testament commands or institutions Jesus set aside?

How did Jesus fulfill the Old Testament?

Day 54

Six Questions to Ask of God's Word

Seeing Jesus at the center of the Scriptures helps us to rightly interpret God's Word today. J. I. Packer lists six questions that we should ask of the biblical text we are studying in order to be faithful interpreters. Use these questions when you are seeking to understand God's Word:

1. What do these words actually mean?

2. What light do other Scriptures throw on this text? Where and how does it fit into the total biblical revelation?

3. What truths does it teach about God and about man in relation to God?

4. How are these truths related to the saving work of Christ, and what light does the gospel of Christ throw upon them?

5. What experiences do these truths delineate or explain or seek to create or cure? For what practical purpose do they stand in Scripture?

6. How do they apply to myself and others in our own actual situation? To what present human condition do they speak, and what are they telling us to believe and do?

Day 55

The Point, Not the Letter

 Imagine that you are the parent of a young child who needs a nap. You put him in bed and say, "Don't get out of bed!" He nods his affirmation as you leave the room. A little while later, you open the door and see him playing in his bed. While you were out, he leaned over to the drawer next to his bed and pulled out a box of Legos to play with. When you confront him, he says, "I didn't get out of bed, did I?" Exasperated, you say, "No, but that wasn't the point. The point was that you needed to get some rest!"

There are all sorts of ways to obey the letter of the law and miss its intention. Kids do it all the time. So do adults. It's easy to become so focused on the rules and regulations that we miss the point. We need the law-giver to remind us of the law's intention.

As the One to whom the Law and the Prophets pointed, Jesus was the faithful interpreter of God's Word. The scribes and Pharisees followed a moralistic interpretation of the law. They were all about the letter of the law, but they had missed the heart.

Do you know of any strange laws still on the books, laws that have outlived their usefulness because their purpose is no longer relevant? Why is it important that we understand God's intentions when we seek to apply the Scriptures?

Jesus Interpreted the Law by Pointing to the Heart of the Author

 Jesus explained the true meaning of the law as God intended. Contrary to what the people had heard, Jesus declared that the intention of the law was not about checking off a list of moral requirements but total obedience that flowed from a pure heart. Anything less excludes one from the kingdom of heaven.

Consider just two examples of Jesus' teaching in relation to God's law.

> *"You have heard that it was said to our ancestors, Do not murder, and whoever murders will be subject to judgment. But I tell you, everyone who is angry with his brother will be subject to judgment. And whoever says to his brother, 'Fool!' will be subject to the Sanhedrin. But whoever says, 'You moron!' will be subject to hellfire." (Matt. 5:21–22)*

The phrase "You have heard that it was said . . . But I tell you . . ." distinguished Jesus' teaching from that of the scribes and Pharisees and established Jesus as the authoritative interpreter of God's Word.

Can you imagine a Christian preacher standing before a congregation and saying, "You've heard Jesus say this, but I tell you . . ."? If you were to hear such a thing, you'd march up to that pastor and ask, "Who do you think you are?" And that's the point. Jesus wasn't just revealing the true interpretation of God's law. He was also revealing His authority to say so. Now back to Jesus' interpretation of the law regarding murder. Clearly the Sixth Commandment declared murder to be against the will of God (Exod. 20:13). We learn in Genesis that the reason murder is forbidden is because humankind is created in God's image (Gen. 1:26–28; 5:1–2); therefore, anyone who kills another human being created in God's image forfeits their own life (9:6).

Unlike the scribes and Pharisees, however, Jesus was not concerned merely with the physical act of murder; He was concerned with the sin of the heart that leads to murder—unrighteous anger. Jesus was not denying that murderers will be judged; that is the law. Jesus was simply saying that murder flows from a sinful heart, and sinners will be judged not only for their sinful actions but also for their sinful attitudes. It is such sinful attitudes that breed a contempt that leads us to call people "fools" or "morons" (see James 3:7–12), and the person whose heart overflows with anger will be damned to hell.

This may sound harsh to us, but it's actually the expression of our Savior's compassionate heart. Why the tough words? Because murder flows from an angry heart. If you don't believe that's true, consider Cain and Abel. God exposed Cain's anger (Gen. 4:6). It was Cain's anger that led him to kill Abel (4:8; see also 1 John 3:11–12). Murder begins in the heart. There are many ways that murderous anger can slowly kill a soul. We murder people by destroying their reputations. We murder people, particularly children, by how we speak to them. Imagine how many children feel inadequate and inept at everything because their entire lives they have been told how stupid they are. Such angry people, says Jesus, will be guilty at the judgment and experience the fire of hell rather than the eternal kingdom (Matt. 5:22).

Examine your heart. Are you harboring bitter thoughts toward people right now?

Have you been angry with someone and not taken steps to reconcile?

Day 57

More Than Just Anger

 We've spent a lot of time on the Sixth Commandment because it is a common struggle for most of us, but we can apply Jesus' teaching to every area of our lives in light of God's law. Let's consider lust.

> *"You have heard that it was said, Do not commit adultery. But I tell you, everyone who looks at a woman to lust for her has already committed adultery with her in his heart." (Matt. 5:27–28)*

We live in a sex-crazed world where sex sells (billboards, magazine ads, commercials, you name it). Unfortunately, the church is not untouched by adultery, which leads to sexual scandal and the tarnishing of our gospel witness in the world.

The religious leaders of Jesus' day thought they were fulfilling the Seventh Commandment simply by avoiding sexual relations with someone who was not their spouse. But Jesus was interested in the heart attitudes that lead to the sinful physical act. The Pharisees seemed to have forgotten the Tenth Commandment: "Do not covet your neighbor's wife" (Exod. 20:17).

In His teaching, Jesus exposed the corruption of the human heart, the seriousness of sin, and the certainty of punishment for lawbreakers. Clearly, when we understand the law as God intended it, we are all shown to be lawbreakers. Jesus taught that we must deal with sin seriously because those who continue in unrepentant sin will be excluded from the kingdom of heaven and experience the fires of hell (Matt. 5:29–30; 7:21–23). Thankfully, this word of judgment leads to the offer of salvation.

What sins do you struggle with?

How are you fighting against sin and temptation?

How do these struggles with sin affect your understanding of whether or not you will enter the kingdom of heaven?

DAY 58

Jesus Laid Out God's Expectations and Then Met Them

 Have you ever been to a theme park? Having moved to Florida as a kid, I grew up going to Disney World's Magic Kingdom. When the park closes in the evening, officials don't check to see if you had a ticket that allowed you to get in. Their main concern is that everyone get out! So they open all their gates and unlock all their turnstiles in order to guide their guests out of the park in an organized but speedy manner. Entrance into the park is a completely different situation. If you want to get into the Magic Kingdom, you must show your ticket (proving that you paid the price of admission) and enter into the park individually through the turnstiles that are guarded by security. No ticket, no entrance.

At stake in Jesus' teaching is entrance into a kingdom. But we're not talking about some temporary escape into a fantastical, magical theme park. No, this is about everlasting inclusion in the kingdom of God, where righteousness dwells.

Jesus accused the scribes and Pharisees of locking people out of God's kingdom (Matt. 23:13). The Pharisees had separated God's law from God's character, leading them to reduce the law to a set of moral rules that were to be followed in legalistic fashion. The idea was that by keeping the rules one could gain entrance into the kingdom. Jesus could not have disagreed more (7:21–23). Instead, Jesus declared that "unless your righteousness surpasses that of the scribes and Pharisees, you will never enter the kingdom of heaven" (5:20).

Since the scribes and the Pharisees were famous for keeping "the law," how could anyone's righteousness surpass theirs? Just what kind of righteousness does God's law require, or in today's terms, "How good is good enough?" Not only did Jesus correctly interpret the law, He also intensified it. How good is good enough? Total perfection.

> "You have heard that it was said, Love your neighbor and hate your enemy. But I tell you, love your enemies and pray for those who persecute you, so that you may be sons of your Father in heaven. For He causes His sun to rise on the evil and the good, and sends rain on the righteous and the unrighteous. For if you love those who love you, what reward will you have? Don't even the tax collectors do the same? And if you greet only your brothers, what are you doing out of the ordinary? Don't even the Gentiles do the same? Be perfect, therefore, as your heavenly Father is perfect." (Matt. 5:43–48)

Did you catch that last verse? The standard of righteousness that God requires is perfection. None of us can meet that standard. God's law reveals the perfect character of God, and perfection is precisely what God expects of us. The problem is that we have all broken God's law. This is the great human dilemma. The good news of the gospel is that Jesus came to fulfill the law. It was Jesus who loved His enemies fully, even praying for those who tormented Him on the cross. It was Jesus who welcomed tax collectors and sinners to His table. It was Jesus who showed us the perfection of the Father. The law has two basic demands. First, the law demands perfect obedience that flows from a pure heart. Because our hearts are corrupt, we cannot fulfill this demand. Jesus, however, could and did by obeying the law at every point; He did not leave out even the smallest, seemingly insignificant parts of the words of the law.

Second, the law also demands the death penalty for lawbreakers. The good news is that Jesus fulfilled this demand by taking upon Himself the curse of the law on our behalf. The death penalty for lawbreaking was administered to Jesus on the cross. Those who gain entrance into the kingdom of heaven, then, are not those who try to work at it but those who trust in Jesus' fulfilling of the law in their place. And those who truly believe will obey Jesus' teaching. Through faith we are enabled to begin living in accordance with Jesus' teaching! As the apostle Paul declared, "the righteous will live by faith" (Gal. 3:11). This is the righteousness that surpasses that of the Pharisees.

How does trusting in Christ's fulfilling work encourage you to have assurance of salvation?

How would you explain the good news of the gospel in terms of Jesus' fulfilling the Law and the Prophets to someone who has never heard it before? To someone who is struggling with assurance of salvation?

The Mission

 The Sermon on the Mount pushes us to the end of ourselves by exposing the corruption of our sinful hearts. When we recognize that Jesus fulfilled the demands of the law perfectly on our behalf, we are transformed. By faith in Jesus, the righteousness of Christ is accounted to us, and the penalty for our breaking the law is accounted to Christ. This is the great exchange! Even better, by faith in Christ, we receive new hearts that allow us to obey all that Jesus taught—to love the Lord our God with every fiber of our being and to love our neighbor as ourselves. This too is a fulfillment of the Law and the Prophets (Jer. 31:31–34; Ezek. 36:24–27).

Now our mission is defined in relation to Jesus' teaching. Since Jesus faithfully fulfilled the Law and the Prophets, the Father has granted Him authority over heaven and earth. As the sovereign King, Jesus commands us to go out under His authority into the world with this good news. Our commission is not simply to baptize but to make disciples by also "teaching them to observe everything" that Jesus commanded (Matt. 28:18–20). Let us therefore embrace Jesus' teaching and tell others what He has taught us.

How does understanding the Great Commission in light of Jesus' teaching help you to fulfill the church's mission to the world as well as help you find your place in God's mission?

Day 60

Jesus: The Faithful Student

 "What would Jesus do?" Though these words may bring back memories of WWJD bracelets in the 1990s, the phrase was actually made popular by Charles Sheldon's classic book *In His Steps*, first published in 1897.

Sheldon's fictional story begins as Reverend Henry Maxwell, pastor of First Church of Raymond, seeks the quiet solitude of his study at home in order to prepare Sunday's sermon on 1 Peter 2:21: "For you were called to this, because Christ also suffered for you, leaving you an example, so that you should follow in His steps." Maxwell is interrupted when a young man in his early thirties, disheveled, dirty, and homeless comes to his door. Anxious to return to his study, the pastor offers little help and wishes him well. Much to Reverend Maxwell's surprise, the same homeless man stands up to speak to the congregation at the end of the sermon on imitating Christ. He asks: "I was wondering, as I sat there under the gallery, if what you call following Jesus is the same thing as what He taught. What did He mean when He said, 'Follow Me'? The minister said . . . that it was necessary for the disciple of Jesus to follow His steps, and he said the steps were obedience, faith, love, and imitation. But I did not hear him tell you just what he meant that to mean, especially the last step. What do Christians mean by following the steps of Jesus?" While still speaking, the young man collapses to the floor. Reverend Maxwell and his wife take him into their home to care for him, but he dies a few days later. Moved by this experience, Maxwell steps into the pulpit on the following Sunday and challenges the congregation: "Our motto will be, 'What would Jesus do?' Our aim will be to act just as He would if He were in our places, regardless of immediate results. In other words, we propose to follow Jesus' steps as closely and as literally as we believe He taught His disciples to do. And those who volunteer to do this will pledge themselves for an entire year, beginning with to-day, so to act."

Though the idea of asking what Jesus would do is good, Christians too often apply this "imitation of Christ" only to ethical situations. The unintended result is that Jesus gets reduced to just a teacher of morals. Of course, it is true that we are called to imitate Christ. But too often, we don't think carefully about what this imitation looks like and what it will cost us.

Imitation of Christ requires meditation on Christ. If we are to know what it means to follow Christ, then we must seek to study Christ—His life and teaching and, most importantly, His death and resurrection. Therefore, if we are to imitate Christ, we need to ask a different question—not just "What would Jesus do?" but "What has Jesus done?" Once we understand what Jesus has done, we can best understand how to represent Him and follow Him faithfully.

*What would it mean to literally
follow "in Christ's steps"?*

What does imitating Christ cost us?

Day 61

Christk Submitted to the Father's Will

 For many people today, *submission* is a dirty word. Our revulsion against submission is rooted in the sinful disposition we inherited from Adam that inclines us to rebel against authority. When Adam sinned, he essentially told God, "Not Your will be done but mine!" Like Adam, we want to be our own kings. We don't like anyone telling us what to do, not even God.

Think about the heroes of many American movies and television shows. Many times, the heroes are those who rebel against authority in pursuit of a greater good.

Jesus came as our substitute. He obeyed God at the very point where Adam rebelled. Let's look at Jesus in the garden of Gethsemane on the night He was betrayed. Again, through great suffering, Jesus chose to obey the Father's word and to submit to His will.

"Then they came to a place named Gethsemane, and He told His disciples, "Sit here while I pray." He took Peter, James, and John with Him, and He began to be deeply distressed and horrified. Then He said to them, "My soul is swallowed up in sorrow—to the point of death. Remain here and stay awake." Then He went a little farther, fell to the ground, and began to pray

that if it were possible, the hour might pass from Him. And He said, "Abba, Father! All things are possible for You. Take this cup away from Me. Nevertheless, not what I will, but what You will." (Mark 14:32–36)

Jesus knew that obeying the Father would bring great suffering. That's why He became so deeply distressed and horrified, such that He told His disciples that He was filled with "sorrow—to the point of death." Jesus' agony was rooted in the knowledge that the time had almost arrived to fulfill the purpose of His death. Jesus did not come in the flesh merely to die; He came to die on behalf of sinners.

Have you ever had to submit to the Father's will knowing it would bring about suffering?

How does understanding the purposes of God allow you to face suffering?

Christ Followed Even into Suffering

 The Bible teaches that those who continue in rebellion to God's Word and refuse to submit to God's will are storing up wrath for themselves. One way the Bible describes the outpouring of God's wrath is with the imagery of a cup filled with wine. The wine represents God's wrath/anger (Jer. 25:15–17, 28; 49:12). On the day of judgment, God will pour out the cup filled with the wine of His wrath, and He will make rebellious sinners drink every last drop until they become drunk with His wrath (Ps. 75:8; Ezek. 23:32–34).

At the cross (the "hour" that Jesus spoke of), God the Father poured out the full cup of His wrath on His own Son as a judgment against sin. Since Jesus took on our sin, He was forsaken and abandoned (Mark 15:34). Anticipating this judgment, Jesus asked His Father, the only One with the authority to remove Him from both this hour and this cup, if there were any possible way that He could alter His will so that His Word could be fulfilled through some other means.

In the end, however, unlike Adam, Jesus submitted to the Father's will with an emphatic "Not what I will, but what You will." Jesus knew that there was no way to fulfill the Father's Word other than to submit to the Father's will. God could only take this cup away from His people by pouring it out on His righteous Servant (Isa. 51:17, 21–22). Jesus received the wounds we deserved, and by faith we receive forgiveness (53:1–12).

Only when we meditate on Christ's life and death (what He has done) are we able to imitate Christ. If we fail to ground our efforts to be like Christ in the good news of what Christ has done for us, we will throw up our hands and give up! The cross is what makes possible our obedience. And the cross shapes what our obedience looks like. This means that we, like Jesus, are to submit to the Father's will, even when it results in suffering. Because we are called to follow Christ, we are called to suffer (1 Pet. 2:21). Don't be surprised when suffering comes your way! This is one way God slowly transforms us into the image of His Son.

The good news is that by His death and resurrection, Jesus has granted us the power to face suffering (vv. 24–25).

How does meditating on Christ help you prepare to face suffering now?

What does a Christlike response to suffering look like?

DAY 63

Christ Submitted to the Father's Will, even though It Brought Great Shame

Make your own attitude that of Christ Jesus, who, existing in the form of God, did not consider equality with God as something to be used for His own advantage. Instead He emptied Himself by assuming the form of a slave, taking on the likeness of men. And when He had come as a man in His external form, He humbled Himself by becoming obedient to the point of death —even to death on a cross. (Phil. 2:5–11)

 Jesus had all the privileges that came with being God. Yet in submitting to the Father's will, He set those privileges aside in order to become human for our salvation. Jesus did not empty Himself of deity; He took on a lowly status and position as He took on humanity. Jesus had to step out of the glories of heaven, become a servant, and take on flesh. According to the Father's plan of redemption, Jesus had to become like us in order to rescue us.

It may be helpful to think of Jesus' humiliation (incarnation) in this context. Imagine a righteous king who creates a special place, a sanctuary, where he and his people can share together in joy, peace, and love. There is no shame in this sanctuary because there is no evil present; there is only fellowship and joy and life. However, the people are not satisfied with serving the righteous king. They want to be their own kings, so they rebel and seek to establish their own kingdoms.

As punishment for rejecting his rule, the king casts the rebels out of the sanctuary and into a dark kingdom ruled by an evil prince who wields the power of death. Without realizing it, the rebels have become slaves of their own rebellion and of the evil prince who uses the fear of death as a weapon against them.

Because the king loves his people, he chooses to rescue them. But since he is a righteous king, he cannot simply overlook their rebellion. Therefore, in order to rescue the rebels, the king must send his righteous son, the heir to the throne, to this dark realm. In submitting to his father, the righteous son must step away from all his royal privileges. But he is still the prince; the royal blood flows through his veins. So in obedience to his father, he enters a different and dark realm where no one acknowledges his authority.

The righteous prince becomes like the captive rebels in order to take their place and rescue them. He obeys all the laws the rebels broke, but he also receives the punishment the rebels deserve. Ultimately the righteous prince must suffer the shame and ridicule of a public trial where the charges against the rebels are read. Then he must face the humiliating, public execution that their crimes require.

Only through the son's obedience can the righteous king and the rebels be reconciled. The Gospel accounts reveal that Jesus is the righteous Prince sent by the righteous King to rescue a rebellious people held captive by the Evil One.

In Philippians 2:5–8, the apostle Paul reminds us that Jesus submitted to the Father's will in humbling Himself in order to rescue us, even though it brought Him great shame. Thankfully our story does not end with Christ's shameful death, for humiliation leads to exaltation.

> *For this reason God highly exalted Him and gave Him the name that is above every name, so that at the name of Jesus every knee should bow—of those who are in heaven and on earth and under the earth— and every tongue should confess that Jesus Christ is Lord, to the glory of God the Father. (vv. 9–11)*

God, the righteous King, raised Jesus from the dead, defeating the evil prince, conquering death, and nullifying the fear of death. In fact, because of Jesus' obedient humiliation, the Father exalted Him to the place of ultimate authority. Jesus was crowned Lord and King over all, and the entire universe will bow down to Him and confess His lordship. He who humbled Himself as a servant became the exalted One through His perfect response to God's Word.

How does having the attitude of Christ (Phil. 2:5) lead to imitating Christ (vv. 3–4)?

Why is it important that we ground our efforts to imitate Christ in the "mind," or "attitude," of Christ?

Are you willing to sacrifice personal comfort in order that others might hear of Christ?

Day 64

Christ's Submission Leads to Our Purification and His Exaltation

 It is fascinating to think how often the theme of exaltation through humiliation in the life of Christ is imitated in art. Living with five daughters, I am all too familiar with the story of Cinderella—the daughter who became a servant, who then became a princess. As a man in a house full of girls, I prefer to watch movies like *Gladiator*, which is about a general who became a slave, who became a gladiator, who became the savior of Rome.

Most recently, my older girls and I went to see the movie *Thor*. (My apologies to comic book purists reading this lesson, but I am going to follow the theatrical story line!) Like other fictional stories, Thor follows the theme of exaltation through humiliation. Thor is the "god" of thunder, whose father is Odin, the wise, righteous king of the planet Asgard—a place resembling a celestial city. Though Thor is destined to be crowned king of Asgard, his arrogance leads Odin to banish him to Earth, where he is stripped of his powers and forced to learn humility. Once the lesson is learned, Thor's god-like powers are returned to him, and he is able to become the hero/savior he was meant to be and return to Asgard to his rightful place next to his father.

All of these stories that people love to tell, generation after generation, are powerful precisely because they follow many of the themes of the true story about our world. The story of God, the righteous King, and His Son, Jesus, is the true story of exaltation through humiliation. All other stories fall short. They pale in comparison to the story of Jesus. Notice how the author of Hebrews sets up the story of Jesus.

> *Long ago God spoke to the fathers by the prophets at different times and in different ways. In these last days, He has spoken to us by His Son. God has appointed Him heir of all things and made the universe through Him. The Son is the radiance of God's glory and the exact expression of His nature, sustaining all things by His powerful word. After making purification for sins, He sat down at the right hand of the Majesty on high. So He became higher in rank than the angels, just as the name He inherited is superior to theirs. (Heb. 1:1–4)*

In order that the world would know Him in all His glory, God has spoken His story to His people throughout history. In the Old Testament era, God spoke through different persons in various, fragmentary ways—fire, smoke, direct word, prophecy, dreams, visions, angels, etc. (Heb. 1:1).

"In these last days" indicates that by His coming, Jesus ushered in the new era of fulfillment that the Old Testament pointed to. In this new era, God has finally and uniquely spoken to us in Jesus Christ, who, as "the radiance of God's glory," is the very presence of God. To know Jesus is to know God; to see Jesus is to see God.

> *In what ways did God speak to His people before Jesus' first coming? In what ways was this revelation only partial?*

Day 65

Jesus Reveals God's Character

 As "the exact expression of His nature," Jesus glorified the Father by revealing the very character of God. It is true that Jesus glorified the Father through His life and ministry. Yet Jesus ultimately and uniquely revealed the character of God in His death and resurrection.

In His death and resurrection, Jesus revealed the Father's justice against human sinfulness and rebellion. At the cross, the Father's righteousness was revealed as He judged sin in Christ; God is both just and the justifier of sinners. Christ's death revealed that God takes sin seriously, and so must we. Forgiveness may be free, but it is not cheap.

In His death and resurrection, Jesus also revealed the Father's power and authority over Satan. Christ came to crush Satan and to set us free from his power. The cross, which at first appears to be Satan's victory, is actually Satan's downfall.

In His death and resurrection, Jesus also revealed the Father's grace and mercy toward undeserving sinners of every ethnicity. By "lifting up" Jesus on the cross, the Father now draws a multi-ethnic people to the Son, a people who are His witnesses to salvation. Now we are commissioned as ambassadors, spreading the good news of His reign to those still in darkness.

Jesus' willing submission to a harsh and shameful death on a cross began His kingly procession to His throne. Once Jesus made purification for sins by receiving the penalty for sin in Himself, His high priestly work was finished, as indicated by the fact that He sat down. Having accomplished His atoning work, Jesus sat down at the right hand of God—the place of honor.

Jesus, the One who humbled Himself by submitting to the Father, is now the exalted One. As the obedient Son, Jesus has inherited everything in the universe, which was made through Him. As the exalted One who is crowned King of kings and Lord of lords (Phil. 2:9–11), Jesus is superior to the angels (Heb. 1:4–5,14; 2:2–3, 18), to Moses (3:1–6; 11:23–29, 39), to Joshua (3:7–4:8), to Aaron (5:4), to Melchizedek (chap. 7), to the priests (chaps. 8–9), to the sacrifices (10:1–18), and yes, even Thor. All glory and honor be to King Jesus!

What do you think is the significance of Jesus sitting "down at the right hand of the Majesty on high" in Hebrews 1:3?

How does Christ's purification of our sin empower us to submit to God's Word?

What should be our response to God's final revelation in Christ?

Knowing that Christ has been exalted, what should be our posture toward Him?

What Will You Do?

Reverend Henry Maxwell, pastor of the fictional First Church of Raymond, was right. We are called to imitate Christ (1 Pet. 2:21). But if we are to imitate Christ, instead of asking, "What would Jesus do?" we should be asking, "What has Jesus done?" By focusing on what Jesus has done, we will be able to see the bigger picture of God's plan to glorify Himself through both the humiliation and exaltation of Jesus Christ.

Asking what Jesus has done also moves us to ask, "Why? Why did Jesus humble Himself, becoming obedient, even unto a harsh and shameful death?" We have seen the answer to this question in today's lesson. By submitting to the Father's will, Jesus revealed the Father's heart of love for His fallen creation. Though we are the rebels in God's story, God has spoken to us of His love, mercy, and grace in Jesus' death. To be sure, God has also spoken to us about His justice and righteousness in Jesus' death as well.

When we realize that God has spoken to us in Jesus Christ, the natural question is "What will be our response?" The appropriate response, of course, is repentance (turning away from our rebellion and our desire to be our own kings) and faith (turning to Christ, bowing down and acknowledging Him as our King).

The good news is that those who trust in Christ are exalted with Christ. However, those who reject Christ's rule will receive the full cup of God's wrath (Col. 3:5–7). So then, the question every person must grapple with is not "What would Jesus do?" but rather "What will you do with Jesus?"

How have you responded to God's revelation of Himself in Jesus?

How are you living your life in light of God's revelation of Himself in Jesus?

Are there people in your life who presently do not bow to King Jesus?

What is your responsibility to share the revelation of God in Jesus Christ to them?

Trusting

Ground-level—that's where life begins. Wide-eyed and full of awe, we spend twelve months crawling on hands and knees. Eventually we learn to stand, to balance, to walk and jog and run. From elliptical machines and ice skates to tennis shoes and roller blades, sooner or later, our abilities increase. However, the taller we grow and the faster we go, the less we return to our knees. In the end, we as adults exchange a world of ground-level for a world of eye-level, and we often forget the beauty of humility.

Stephen knew something about "ground-level." As the first Christian martyr, Stephen proclaimed with great boldness the faith that eventually cost his life. Although his name means "crown," Stephen understood that Christ's followers cannot wear the crown without carrying the cross. For him, like all Christians, the way up is the way down. Jesus once said, "If anyone wants to come with Me, he must deny himself, take up his cross, and follow Me" (Matt. 16:24). Following in the footsteps of his Savior, Stephen knew that faithfulness before God is more important than popularity before men. He knew that the proper posture toward God's Holy Word is repentance for sin and trust in Jesus Christ.

Stephen returned to his knees—physically and spiritually. And then God worked powerfully through

Stephen's life and witness. Stephen's testimony offers us a 3-D Christianity. He shows us that following Jesus Christ involves three dimensions: information, transformation, and proclamation. Stephen believed the good news about Christ (information), loved Christ (transformation), and preached Christ (proclamation). Likewise, we have the opportunity to give our heads, hearts, and lips to the God who creates us and re-creates us.

Which of these dimensions (believing in Christ, loving Christ, preaching Christ) do you find easiest? Which do you find most difficult? Why?

DAY 68

Stephen Demonstrated Knowledge of God's Word

Let's look at Stephen's sermon in Acts 7:2–16.

"Brothers and fathers," he said, "listen: The God of glory appeared to our father Abraham when he was in Mesopotamia, before he settled in Haran, and said to him: Get out of your country and away from your relatives, and come to the land that I will show you. "Then he came out of the land of the Chaldeans and settled in Haran. From there, after his father died, God had him move to this land you now live in. He didn't give him an inheritance in it, not even a foot of ground, but He promised to give it to him as a possession, and to his descendants after him, even though he was childless. God spoke in this way: His descendants would be strangers in a foreign country, and they would enslave and oppress them for 400 years. I will judge the nation that they will serve as slaves, God said. After this, they will come out and worship Me in this place. Then He gave him the covenant of circumcision. After this, he fathered Isaac and circumcised him on the eighth day; Isaac did the same with Jacob, and Jacob with the 12 patriarchs. "The patriarchs became jealous of Joseph and sold him into Egypt, but God was with him and rescued him

out of all his troubles. He gave him favor and wisdom in the sight of Pharaoh, king of Egypt, who appointed him ruler over Egypt and over his whole household. Then a famine and great suffering came over all of Egypt and Canaan, and our ancestors could find no food. When Jacob heard there was grain in Egypt, he sent our ancestors the first time. The second time, Joseph was revealed to his brothers, and Joseph's family became known to Pharaoh. Joseph then invited his father Jacob and all his relatives, 75 people in all, and Jacob went down to Egypt. He and our ancestors died there, were carried back to Shechem, and were placed in the tomb that Abraham had bought for a sum of silver from the sons of Hamor in Shechem."

Bible memory is vitally important for believers, and it's not merely because we need to know a few isolated verses. Easy recall of the grand narrative of Scripture is life-transforming. Knowing the big picture of the story the Bible tells is what transforms our worldview so that we are able to look at the world through Bible-shaped eyes.

Notice how easily Stephen recalled the details of his people's history. He stood on the promises God had made to Abraham. He recognized the nature of the covenant. He even knew the number of people in Joseph's family who migrated to Egypt (75 to be exact!). Stephen knew the Bible as a whole and in its parts, and that's why his sermon was so powerful. The Bible is powerful, which is why the apostle Paul likened it to a sword. Jesus turned to the Word when He was tempted in the wilderness.

There were no "amens" or "hallelujahs" at the end of Stephen's sermon. In fact, instead of listening for long, his audience reached for weapons to kill him. Beginning with Abraham, Isaac, and Jacob, Stephen presented a panorama of the Old Testament. He explained the history of the Israelites, Joseph's slavery in Egypt, and the Israelites' exodus to the promised land. Stephen knew his Bible backwards and forwards. And his sermon teaches an important truth about God's Word. When difficulty comes, the testimonies of Scripture encourage and remind God's people of God's faithfulness.

Do you set aside time to spend with Scripture?

Do you set aside space where you open your Bible and listen to God from His Word?

Day 69

Stephen Demonstrated His Trust in the Truth of God's Word

However, the Most High does not dwell in sanctuaries made with hands, as the prophet says: Heaven is My throne, and earth My footstool. What sort of house will you build for Me? says the Lord, or what is My resting place? Did not My hand make all these things? You stiff-necked people with uncircumcised hearts and ears! You are always resisting the Holy Spirit; as your ancestors did, so do you. (Acts 7:48–51)

 Jesus once compared the Holy Spirit to the wind that "blows where it pleases" (John 3:8). It was this same Spirit that hovered over the surface of the waters (Gen. 1:2), that breathed life into Adam's lungs, and that inspired the writers of the Bible—"Men spoke from God," wrote Peter, "as they were moved by the Holy Spirit" (2 Pet. 1:21). Theologians call this concept *inspiration*. It's the idea that God divinely inspired His Word. Make no mistake about it, God is the ultimate Author of His Book. But God enlisted a variety of writers to pen His words.

In Stephen's sermon, we see that he took for granted the origin of the Bible. He knew sure enough that it came from God through men. Yet he also took for granted the veracity

134

of the biblical account. Notice in this passage how he clearly assumes the factual nature of the Bible's story line. Moving from Moses to Joshua to Solomon, Stephen's sermon builds upon the solid foundation of biblical teaching and climaxes with a clear diagnosis of his listeners' resistance to the Holy Spirit.

As Christians, we submit to the Holy Spirit as He speaks to us through His Word. Everything that God tells us in the Bible is true. We call this the doctrine of inerrancy. Paul tells us in 2 Timothy 3:16 that the Bible is "God-breathed" (NIV). What does this mean? It means that God's Word originates from God's breath. Those who deny inerrancy are saying, in effect, that God has breathed out something false, something impure. Instead, God's breath is pure, holy, flawless, and true. If God breathes something into existence, whether it's a word or a world, in its original form it's going to come out perfect.

Because God's Word is inspired, inerrant, and authoritative, you and I can lean hard against it. Like Stephen, we can trust Scripture, believing that what the Bible says happened really happened. God discloses His nature and character to us in His Word. It follows that the better we know the Bible, the better we know the God of the Bible.

In what ways can our knowledge of Scripture influence the way we worship God, both privately and corporately?

DAY 70

Stephen Spoke the Truth with Boldness

"Which of the prophets did your fathers not persecute? They even killed those who announced beforehand the coming of the Righteous One, whose betrayers and murderers you have now become. You received the law under the direction of angels and yet have not kept it." When they heard these things, they were enraged in their hearts and gnashed their teeth at him. But Stephen, filled by the Holy Spirit, gazed into heaven. He saw God's glory, with Jesus standing at the right hand of God, and he said, "Look! I see the heavens opened and the Son of Man standing at the right hand of God!" Then they screamed at the top of their voices, covered their ears, and together rushed against him. They threw him out of the city and began to stone him. And the witnesses laid their robes at the feet of a young man named Saul. They were stoning Stephen as he called out: "Lord Jesus, receive my spirit!" Then he knelt down and cried out with a loud voice, "Lord, do not charge them with this sin!" And saying this, he fell asleep." (Acts 7:52–60)

We live in a Scripture-saturated society. We've got dozens of translations and dozens of covers:

136

brown leather, alligator leather, olive wood, Velcro, duct tape. We produce Bibles for preschoolers, college students, young adults, apologists, archaeologists, athletes. We buy one-year Bibles, interlinear Bibles, amplified, simplified, limited edition Bibles.

Christians have so many Bible options that we take them for granted; we often devalue them and neglect to read them. Here's the question: How can we make sure that the Scriptures that come into our hands also come out of our mouths?

Stephen shows us how to recover a reverent posture before Scripture. His testimony teaches us that the Bible isn't just another book that sits on our shelves but the greatest love story ever told, one that begins and ends with a gracious God bent on pursuing and redeeming His people. Stephen shows us that knowing God with our heads is not enough. Even the demons know there is one God (James 2:19). Rather, Stephen teaches us that knowledge of God never remains in the abstract. Knowledge must become trust. Trust must become love. And just as when you love someone, you cannot help but talk about Him. You cannot help but talk to Him. And that is the place where God's pursuit of us becomes our witness for Him, a place where transformation leads to proclamation.

*How essential to following Christ
is "sharing the gospel"?*

*Why is the vocalizing of faith so important
for citizens of God's kingdom?*

Day 71

God's Word Is Priceless

For the word of God is living and effective and sharper than any double-edged sword, penetrating as far as the separation of soul and spirit, joints and marrow. It is able to judge the ideas and thoughts of the heart. (Heb. 4:12)

"In the eighteenth year of King Josiah, the king sent the court secretary Shaphan son of Azaliah, son of Meshullam, to the LORD's temple, saying, "Go up to Hilkiah the high priest so that he may total up the money brought into the LORD's temple—the money the doorkeepers have collected from the people. It is to be put into the hands of those doing the work—those who oversee the LORD's temple. They in turn are to give it to the workmen in the LORD's temple to repair the damage. They are to give it to the carpenters, builders, and masons to buy timber and quarried stone to repair the temple. But no accounting is to be required from them for the money put into their hands since they work with integrity." Hilkiah the high priest told Shaphan the court secretary, "I have found the book of the law in the LORD's temple," and he gave the book to Shaphan, who read it. Then Shaphan the court secretary went to the king and reported, "Your

servants have emptied out the money that was found in the temple and have put it into the hand of those doing the work—those who oversee the LORD's temple." Then Shaphan the court secretary told the king, "Hilkiah the priest has given me a book," and Shaphan read it in the presence of the king." (2 Kings 22:3–10)

 In 1902, a paleontologist named Barnum Brown made a surprising discovery in Hell Creek, Montana. Later named the "world's greatest dinosaur hunter," Brown unearthed the skeleton of a "large Carnivorous Dinosaur." He unearthed a second, fuller specimen in 1908. Unlike other dinosaurs he discovered, this forty-five-foot-long monster (aka Tyrannosaurus rex) was a "king of the period and a monarch of its race," boasting a four-foot-long skull with six-inch-long teeth. It was the greatest discovery of his life, a discovery that forever changed the way dinosaurs were studied in the future.

Almost three thousand years earlier, a high priest named Hilkiah also made an important discovery. During the renovation of Solomon's temple, Hilkiah stumbled upon a scroll that had been hidden for centuries. This was no ordinary manuscript. To Hilkiah's surprise, the scroll happened to be the long-lost Book of the Law, the writings that Moses passed down to Joshua (see Josh. 1:6–8).

Would your attitude toward Scripture change if it were extremely difficult to obtain a copy? How so?

What if it were illegal to own a copy of the Bible?

God's Word Is Timeless

We live in a culture of upgrades. Take, for instance, the faithful laptop these words were written on. A MacBook Pro, 2.66 GHz, Intel Core 2 Duo. A fine piece of machinery, for sure. But an outdated one. There's always something faster on the market, something newer. Our culture values upgrading, and whether it's the latest iPhone or the latest fashion, new things seem to have authority over old things. C. S. Lewis once said that some things in this world are permanent and eternal. He called them "first things."

King Josiah understood that God's Word was a first thing, a primary thing that contains truth that transcends time and place. When Josiah heard about the discovery of the scroll, he understood its significance and ordered Shaphan, the secretary of the court, to read it aloud in Josiah's presence. Josiah's response to the discovery of the scroll teaches us that the Word of God is our final authority, the standard by which all things are judged—even us. The Bible is old, but the Bible never gets old. You and I can examine and scrutinize the Scriptures, but God's Word also examines and scrutinizes us. Since God is the Author of His Word, to disobey or disbelieve Scripture is to disobey and disbelieve God.

Pastor Joshua Harris writes:

> *The doctrine of Scripture teaches us about the authority of God's Word. Scripture must be the final*

rule of faith and practice for our lives. Not our feelings or emotions. Not signs or prophetic words or hunches. What more can God give us than what he's given in Scripture? The question is, will we listen? Will we obey when we don't like what the Bible has to say?

This is a moment when our belief about Scripture meets reality. What we say we believe makes very little difference until we act on our belief. I suppose most Christians would say that the Bible is the authoritative Word of God. But until this authority actually changes how we live—how we think and act—talk of the authority of Scripture is nothing but a bunch of religious lingo. We're treating the God-breathed Word of God like a lot of hot air.[7]

When push comes to shove, we show what we really believe about the Bible by how we act. We can say that we believe the Bible is true and authoritative and therefore we are to submit to it, but what we affirm about God's Word can be denied by actions that undercut the Bible's authoritativeness. If the Bible is true and if it is truly authoritative, it must change the way we live.

What would you say to someone who thinks Scripture is just an outdated book—a dinosaur—that might have been powerful long ago but lacks relevance today?

In what areas do you struggle to recognize God's authority?

---

7. Joshua Harris, *Dug Down Deep* (Colorado Springs, CO: Multnomah Books, 2010), 65–66).

DAY 73

God's Word Cuts with Power

For the word of God is living and effective and sharper than any double-edged sword, penetrating as far as the separation of soul and spirit, joints and marrow. It is able to judge the ideas and thoughts of the heart. (Heb. 4:12)

When the king heard the words of the book of the law, he tore his clothes. Then he commanded Hilkiah the priest, Ahikam son of Shaphan, Achbor son of Micaiah, Shaphan the court secretary, and the king's servant Asaiah: "Go and inquire of the LORD for me, the people, and all Judah about the instruction in this book that has been found. For great is the LORD's wrath that is kindled against us because our ancestors have not obeyed the words of this book in order to do everything written about us. (2 Kings 22:11–13)

 In feudal Japan, it could take up to a whole year for a blacksmith to forge a single samurai sword. Unlike Roman, Viking, or Arabian swords, the katana (also called "Japanese steel") was heated and folded thousands of times until most of the impurities were hammered out. That's why the samurai sword could slice through anything in its path.

The author of Hebrews tells us that God's Word is "sharper than any double-edged sword, penetrating as far as the separation of soul and spirit, joints and marrow" (4:12). Although it could take a full year to forge a samurai sword, God spent more than two thousand years forging His Holy Word—a pure and perfect weapon without flaw or impurity.

We call this truth the infallibility of Scripture. It's the idea that God's Word is pure in its authority and authoritative in its purity. In other words, God's weapon contains no deficiencies inherent to its design, construction, and effectiveness. It pierces its target every time, for God said, "My word that comes from My mouth will not return to Me empty, but it will accomplish what I please and will prosper in what I send it to do" (Isa. 55:11).

Jesus once said that the "mouth speaks from the overflow of the heart" (Luke 6:45). Because God's Word flows from God's heart, we can be confident that the Bible is the ultimate standard of truth. When John was on the Isle of Patmos, he saw an image of Jesus Christ with a double-edged sword emerging from His mouth (Rev. 1:16).

What does this tell us about the power
of the Word of God to judge?

Day 74

God's Word Cuts to the Heart of Our Sinful Condition

 The "sword of the Spirit, which is God's word" (Eph. 6:17) is a powerful weapon against Satan (see Matt. 4:1–11), but it is also capable of piercing the hearts of God's people. Look at Acts 2:37. After Peter proclaimed the gospel to the crowd, "they came under deep conviction," and they repented.

The same thing happened to King Josiah after he heard the reading of God's Word. Having realized that his people had provoked God to wrath by not keeping the laws of God, Josiah tore his clothes, a sign of humility and repentance.

The tearing of Josiah's clothes foreshadowed a future event when the Roman soldiers tore up and "divided [Christ's] clothes" (Luke 23:34). Jesus embodied a spirit of humility. We see it not only in His words—"I am gentle and humble in heart" (11:29)—but also in His actions, for "He humbled Himself by becoming obedient to the point of death—even to death on a cross" (Phil. 2:8).

Both Josiah's and Jesus' clothes were torn. However, the tearing of Christ's clothes was not out of repentance but rather out of forgiveness: "Father, forgive them," said Jesus, "because they do not know what they are doing" (Luke 23:34). Amazing love!

Two thousand years later, the Holy Spirit continues to remind us of this event by convicting us of our sins and using God's samurai-sharp Word to penetrate our hearts, judge our thoughts, remove our impurities, and bring us to a place of repentance and ultimate healing in Jesus.

The perfect Word of God shows us our imperfections and gives us a true diagnosis of our fallen state. Whereas the world often tells us that our problem is failing to believe in ourselves, the Bible gives us a stark picture of our true state: we are in rebellion against God. In this way, the Bible cuts to the heart of our sinful condition.

It may be appealing to agree with the world and to think we're not as bad as the Bible says we are, but as Trevin Wax points out in *Confederate Gospel*, this watered-down understanding of sin actually robs us of the beauty of God's grace. "When sin is seen as the rebellion it is, grace is costly—and transformative! When sin is shrunken to the point that our accountability to God is removed, then grace is cheap, and it leaves us unchanged." We need the Word of God to provide us with the stark reality of our fallen condition. Ignoring the Bible's teaching about sin is like ignoring a serious diagnosis from an expert doctor. But thankfully the Bible doesn't just tell us about our fallen state, it also leads us to the prescription: repentance and faith.

Do you read the Bible merely out of habit or do you expect the Lord to convict you of sin and bring you to repentance through His Word?

Give examples of when God's Word has cut to your heart and convicted you of sin in your life.

DAY 75

God's Word Sees All

"No creature is hidden from Him, but all things are naked and exposed to the eyes of Him to whom we must give an account." (Heb. 4:13)

 Controversial as they might be, backscatter X-ray detectors have become the latest advance in airport security. Also known as the "whole body imager" (WBI), this machine detects ionized radiation reflected from objects and then creates a three-dimensional image of those objects.

In other words, if you've got a gun in an airport, the WBI is going to see it. The author of Hebrews says, "all things are naked and exposed to the eyes of Him to whom we must give an account" (4:13). All things. That means you—and me!

Job said, "For His eyes watch over a man's ways, and He observes all his steps. There is no darkness, no deep darkness, where evildoers can hide themselves" (Job 34:21–22). God sees through all of us all of the time. Every thought, every action, every hidden sin and secret is known and perfectly perceived by the all-knowing eye of the Almighty. It is a dangerous thing to stand naked in the presence of a powerful God. Isaiah discovered this to be true when he looked up and "saw the Lord seated on a high and lofty throne, and His robe filled the temple" (Isa. 6:1). What was the first thing out of Isaiah's mouth? "Woe is me for I am ruined because I am a man of unclean lips" (v. 5). In the presence of God, even the angelic seraphim had to shield themselves from God's glorious light.

> *Read Psalm 139. Pay attention to the verbs*
> *in this passage. What do these words reveal*
> *about the abilities and power of God?*

Day 76

God's Word Brings Us to Repentance

 King Josiah knew that unless he humbled himself before the presence of God on behalf of his people, God would destroy them. A day of reckoning was coming. But when God saw Josiah's repentance, He said, "because you have torn your clothes and wept before Me, I Myself have heard you" (2 Kings 22:19). The joy of salvation is that God does not look at His people without a filter.

Instead, the Father sees believers through the lens of Jesus Christ's righteousness. The Messiah's atonement shields us from the wrath of God. Despite our manifold sins and our rebellious natures, God is "patient . . . not wanting any to perish, but all to come to repentance" (2 Pet. 3:9).

Jesus once said, "Unless you repent, you will all perish" (Luke 13:3, 5). The Greek word for "repent" in this passage can be broken into two words: *meta* (a preposition that means "after" or "with") and *noeo* (a verb that means "to think" or "to perceive"). When these two words are combined, the compound word connotes a significant shift of thinking and action, a dynamic "changing of one's mind."

How would you define "repent"? Compare Ezekiel 33:11 and Matthew 12:41. Who are the recipients of each command to repent? What does this suggest about God's ultimate plan of redemption?

DAY 77

Absolute Authority

 Of whom did Jesus say, "I have not found so great a faith even in Israel!" (Luke 7:9)? Was it Peter, James, or John? Perhaps it was Mary or Martha. No. This honor went to a random officer in the Roman army, a centurion. We don't know much about this centurion; in fact, we don't even know his name. But what we do know is that this Roman officer recognized the authority of Jesus better than anyone else Jesus had met, even the disciples.

When the centurion's slave was sick, he sent his friends to tell Jesus, "Lord, don't trouble Yourself, since I am not worthy to have You come under my roof. That is why I didn't even consider myself worthy to come to You. But say the word, and my servant will be cured. For I too am a man placed under authority, having soldiers under my command. I say to this one, 'Go!' and he goes; and to another, 'Come!' and he comes; and to my slave, 'Do this!' and he does it" (vv. 6–8).

Why did Christ pay him the compliment "I have not found so great a faith even in Israel!"? Because this centurion knew the answer to the question "By what authority?" By what authority can my sick slave become well again? Not by Satan's authority. Not by Caesar's authority. Not by tradition's authority. Not even by religion's authority. The supreme authority in heaven and earth belongs to God alone.

Ultimate authority does not come from man-made institutions. It does not come from power, wealth, social status, or reputation. It certainly doesn't come from an ability to grow out a mustache! Instead, all authority under heaven and earth belongs to God, and you and I submit to the God who speaks by reading and obeying the Word He has spoken.

Is the Bible the only source of authority for a Christian or the supreme authority?

How can we distinguish among scriptural authority, conventional wisdom, and false religious teaching?

DAY 78

Understanding

 What would you think if I told you that you were an alien? Not the scaly green kind with big foreheads but the biblical kind, the kind Peter talked about when he reminded the Christians living in Asia Minor that they were "strangers and temporary residents" (1 Pet. 2:11)? To be an alien, in the biblical sense, is to belong to another land. It's the idea that our ultimate citizenship belongs to another Kingdom, to another King.

The Bible consistently teaches that Christians are a sojourning society, traveling from one world to the next. God has given His Word to His traveling pilgrims—the Holy Scripture. In it we discover how to travel, where to travel, and the ways in which we can bring others along on the journey. But the Scriptures must be interpreted correctly in order for it to make sense. Written in the contexts of numerous empires and eras, the biblical writers differed greatly from one another. There were humble shepherds like David and wise sages like Solomon, simple fishermen like Peter and educated scholars like Paul.

Failing to understand each writer and the context, genre, and purpose of such writings can lead not only to a skewed understanding of Scripture but also to unnecessary heartache, confusion, and misdirection.

Over the next few days we will be looking at the four genres of Scripture that will help us interpret God's Word responsibly: historical narrative, wisdom literature, prophecy, and letters. By focusing on these four styles of writing, we can acquire several principles and guidelines in order to understand not only a particular passage of Scripture but also how that passage fits into the overarching narrative of God's redeeming plans.

How does reminding yourself that this is not your home change your behaviors?

Interpreting Historical Narrative

"When Rachel saw that she was not bearing Jacob any children, she envied her sister. "Give me sons, or I will die!" she said to Jacob. Jacob became angry with Rachel and said, "Am I in God's place, who has withheld children from you?" Then she said, "Here is my slave Bilhah. Go sleep with her, and she'll bear children for me so that through her I too can build a family." So Rachel gave her slave Bilhah to Jacob as a wife, and he slept with her. Bilhah conceived and bore Jacob a son. Rachel said, "God has vindicated me; yes, He has heard me and given me a son," and she named him Dan." (Gen. 30:1–6)

 A Sunday school teacher in Nebraska once asked a group of fourth-graders, "What is the hardest commandment for you to keep?" One replied, "Thou shalt not commit adultery." When asked what adultery meant, he explained, "It means 'Do not talk back to adults.'" Misunderstanding the words of Scripture is not merely a fourth-grade problem. Adults can fail to understand them too. And in some cases, the outcome of this misunderstanding can be heartbreaking.

In January 2011, twenty-eight-year-old John Joe Thomas read Leviticus 20:13 and then acted on his reading by stoning to death a seventy-year-old man. Charged with first-degree murder, Thomas claimed that his reading of the Old Testament compelled him to do it. Stories like these are extreme, but they serve to remind us of the importance of rightly interpreting God's Word.

In the passage above, we read an R-rated narrative in which Jacob's wife Rachel cannot become pregnant. So she tells her husband to commit adultery with Bilhah, her slave. Jacob obeys his wife and sleeps with Bilhah, who becomes pregnant with two sons, Dan and Naphtali.

For us to interpret this passage correctly, we need to understand the genre of historical narrative. Approximately 60 percent of the Bible is historical narrative. Sidney Greidanus says historical narrative is the "central, foundational, and all-encompassing genre of the Bible." The purpose of historical narrative literature is simply to narrate, to tell a story.

The Bible contains stories of encouragement and depression, sorrows and celebrations. The characters are many. There is Solomon in his sanctuary and Daniel in his den, Jonah in his whale and Paul in his prison. The plots are unpredictable—a slave who became powerful in Egypt; a shepherd who became king of Israel. Some of these stories reflect the faithfulness of God's people, while others reflect the consequences of neglecting to obey God.

Rachel's story reflects the disobedience of neglecting God's standard. Rachel "envied her sister" because of her sons. Just as Eve tempted Adam and Adam succumbed to her temptation, so Rachel sparked in Jacob's mind a sin that caused them both to stray from God's holy standard.

This story was included in the canon of Scripture to describe the events of Jacob's life, not to encourage us to follow in his sin. It is vitally important to understand the context of a historical narrative. There are three primary kinds of context: (1) Immediate context—the words, phrases, sentences, and paragraphs immediately surrounding the biblical text; (2) Remote context—the chapters and sections surrounding the biblical text; (3) and historical context—the historical setting in which the biblical text was written. Each of these contexts is important in determining how to interpret a particular passage in Scripture.

What is the immediate, remote, and historical context of Genesis 30:1–6?

How does knowing the context help us interpret and apply the individual story?

Interpreting Wisdom Literature

"Teach a youth about the way he should go; even when he is old he will not depart from it." (Prov. 22:6)

"Don't answer a fool according to his foolishness or you'll be like him yourself. Answer a fool according to his foolishness or he'll become wise in his own eyes." (Prov. 26:4–5)

 Jill's parents did everything right. They raised their daughter according to the truths of Scripture. Prayers before meals; prayers before bed. Church three times a week. During the summer, Jill attended church-sponsored camps where she memorized Bible verses. During the semester, she attended a top-tier private Christian school.

In college, Jill renounced any faith she might have had and intentionally distanced herself from church. Expelled for drug and alcohol use, she moved in to live with her boyfriend. Jill's parents were shocked. "What have we done wrong?" they asked. "Why has Jill rejected the God we raised her to love?" Church friends quietly whispered about Jill's parents' failure to raise a good child. After all, Proverbs 22:6 says, "Teach a youth about the way he should go; even when he is old he will not depart from it." If Jill departed, it must mean her parents failed. Good parenting in, good kids out, right? Not so fast.

Interpreting the proverbs as promises is a critical mistake that can fuel legalism, moralism, and disillusionment. Once again, we see the importance of knowing how to interpret the different genres of Scripture and the heartache that comes from a misguided interpretation.

The book of Proverbs is a collection of wise sayings that is categorized under the umbrella of wisdom literature. Unlike the genre of historical narrative that purposes to tell a story, wisdom literature provides general truths about living in a way that honors God.

A proverb is a pithy and persuasive statement or series of statements that has been proven true by experience. However, proverbs are not proven true in every case.

For instance, Proverbs 3:1–3 says that if you obey the commandments in Scripture, "they will bring you many days, a full life." This doesn't mean that all Christians who obey God's commandments will live into their late 70s and 80s. Instead, it means that if you live a life of discipline (1:2), avoid falling into sexual promiscuity (2:16–19), maintain character and integrity in your relationships (3:29–30), and guard your lips from lies (4:24), then it is generally true that the pitfalls that come from sinful actions will escape you. Not always though. Sometimes obeying God's commandments can directly lead to premature death.

Take Stephen, for instance. After being faithful to Christ's instructions to preach the gospel to all nations (Mark 16:15), Stephen boldly proclaimed God's truth and was stoned to death (Acts 7:54–60). Proverbs are general truths. We need to interpret them in that way.

Likewise, we cannot pull one proverb out of context and apply it universally. The two proverbs in Proverbs 26:4–5 appear to contradict one another until you realize that the author is referring to different circumstances. Sometimes it's best to speak to the fool; other times it's best to stay silent.

Like the book of Proverbs, the other books of wisdom literature (Job, Psalms, Song of Songs, and Ecclesiastes) must be interpreted according to their individual purposes. Whereas Job sheds light on the proper relationship between God and people, Psalms contains a variety of purposes: lament and petition, thanksgiving and praise, exaltation of the king, and expressions of trust. These purposes must be interpreted according to each individual category within the Psalms.

At first glance, some verses in the Song of Songs may be interpreted to promote promiscuity (Song of Songs 4:5); however, when they are interpreted in the context of marriage, they illustrate the beauty of intimacy shared between a husband and his bride, beauty that points forward to the relationship between Christ and His church.

What about Ecclesiastes? The purpose of Ecclesiastes is to show us by negative example how best to behave. For instance, when the author says, "Everything is futile" (Eccl. 1:2), we must interpret this in light of other Scripture verses that explain the true meaning and ultimate value of living a godly life (Rom. 12:2; 15:14; Eph. 5:8; 2 Pet. 1:3–11).

Here's the bottom line: misinterpreting wisdom literature can point us in the wrong direction, away from a life that honors and glorifies God. Jill never returned to the faith she was raised to observe . . . at least not yet. But who knows?

Like the prodigal son who "came to his senses," Proverbs 22:6 might just prove to be true in Jill's case after all.

What are some other proverbs that are generally true and yet not applicable to every circumstance?

What are some verses of wisdom literature that you have struggled to interpret correctly?

Interpreting Prophecy

"After this I will pour out My Spirit on all humanity;
then your sons and your daughters will prophesy, your
old men will have dreams, and your young men will
see visions. I will even pour out My Spirit on the male
and female slaves in those days. I will display wonders
in the heavens and on the earth: blood, fire, and
columns of smoke. The sun will be turned to darkness
and the moon to blood before the great and awe-
inspiring Day of the LORD comes." (Joel 2:28–31)

 On May 21, 2011, the followers of "prophet" Harold Camping turned their eyes to the skies in anticipation of the Second Coming of Jesus. These individuals had sold possessions, listed houses on the market, given large sums of money to the doomsday campaign, and even found suitable homes for beloved pets. Jesus was coming back. They had to be ready. On May 22, the "prophet" turned out to be false. But how?

In his Bible, Camping had read Genesis 7:4, "Seven days from now I will make it rain on the earth," and also 2 Peter 3:8, "With the Lord one day is like a thousand years, and a thousand years like one day." From these two passages he concluded that Christ's return would occur exactly 7,000 years after Noah's flood (4990 BC). All that was left to do was the math. 2011 + 4990 – 1 (there is no year between 1 BC and AD 1) = 7,000. Right? Wrong. Jesus did not return on May 21, and the false prophet went into hiding.

Of all the genres of Scripture, prophecy is one of the most difficult to understand, interpret, and apply to our lives. The first step in correctly interpreting prophetic literature is to seek to understand what the author sought to communicate to his original audience. Sometime between 900 BC and 400 BC, a massive swarm of locusts infiltrated Judah. We don't know how widespread this plague was, but in 1889, it was reported that one swarm of locusts crossed the Red Sea and covered a staggering 2,000 square miles. The locusts wreaked havoc on Judah's vegetation and livestock. "Powerful and without number" (Joel 1:6), these creatures destroyed fields, devastated grapevines, stripped bark from trees, withered orchards, and blocked out the rays of the sun over the land.

Against the backdrop of this devastating plague, Joel urged God's people to repent by tearing not just their clothes but also their hearts (2:13). "Who knows?" Joel pondered, "[God] may turn and relent and leave a blessing behind Him" (v. 14). And that's exactly what happened.

Read Deuteronomy 13:1–5 and 18:21–22. According to these Bible passages, what distinguishes a true prophet from a false prophet?

Day 82

Interpreting Letters

"Paul, an apostle—not from men or by man, but by Jesus Christ and God the Father who raised Him from the dead— and all the brothers who are with me: To the churches of Galatia. Grace to you and peace from God the Father and our Lord Jesus Christ, who gave Himself for our sins to rescue us from this present evil age, according to the will of our God and Father. To whom be the glory forever and ever. Amen. I am amazed that you are so quickly turning away from Him who called you by the grace of Christ and are turning to a different gospel—not that there is another gospel, but there are some who are troubling you and want to change the good news about the Messiah." (Gal. 1:1–7)

 Picture yourself driving to work, not necessarily paying attention to your speed. Suddenly you see in your rearview mirror the dreaded flash of red and blue. Most of us have been in that situation. In fact, over 34 million tickets are issued each year (nearly 100,000 daily). Failure to abide by these laws contributes to over 10,000 deaths every year. The letters (also called epistles) constitute a major section in the New Testament. Similar to an e-mail that you might write to a friend or a group of friends, each letter has a particular author and audience.

Take Galatians, for instance, written by Paul to the churches in Galatia around AD 50. It's a short letter, only six chapters long. It includes an introduction, a description of Paul's apostleship, a treatise on the relationship between grace and the law, an appeal, a thesis on what it means to be free in Jesus Christ, and a conclusion. Its primary purpose is to encourage Christians to return to the gospel that they have abandoned.

The Galatians didn't understand how to obey the law—not the traffic law but the law of God. "I am amazed that you are so quickly turning away from Him who called you by the grace of Christ and are turning to a different gospel," wrote Paul (1:6). That's why Paul spent so many words explaining the importance of the law and how the law must be obeyed in relationship to the gospel of grace.

In essence, the churches in Galatia thought that simply obeying the law was enough. By going the speed limit, so to speak, they thought God would be honored with their lives and save them. What they didn't understand was that God desires more than just outward obedience; He desires inward transformation that results in outward obedience.

After the author, audience, and structure of an epistle are established, we can then proceed to discover its meaning for our lives. But we must do so carefully, for some teachings in the Bible are culturally mandated to specific audiences.

For instance, in 1 Corinthians 11:6, Paul writes, "If a woman's head is not covered, her hair should be cut off." Is the application of this text to mean that the women in our churches should wear hats to church every week or else shave their heads? Not necessarily. The church in Corinth would have understood completely that Paul was giving this instruction because prostitutes in the city of Corinth would identify themselves by displaying their long hair in public. Paul wanted to make it very clear that Christian women must act differently than the world. So the application of this passage lies in the principle behind what Paul was saying— modesty—not hair length and accessories.

Determining which texts are culturally mandated can be challenging, and Bible-loving people disagree often. Nevertheless, using this guide to escort us through Scripture as a way to understand the epistles will give greater clarity about how to apply God's Word to your life.

What are some ways in which ancient letters are different from the letters we write today? What are some similarities?

How does knowledge of ancient letter writing help us understand the New Testament letters?

Day 83

Jesus Does Not Leave Us to Ourselves

Two men were traveling by foot from Jerusalem to Emmaus. They were talking about the crucifixion of Jesus when suddenly Jesus joined them on their journey. As they walked, the conversation turned to Scripture.

Then beginning with Moses and all the Prophets, He interpreted for them the things concerning Himself in all the Scriptures. (Luke 24:27)

In essence, the great Teacher gave them a proper understanding of how God speaks through His Word. God's people were never meant to walk in this world alone. We are pilgrims who require God's guidance.

When it comes to interpreting the Word of God, Jesus does not leave us to ourselves. He does not want us to experience the unnecessary heartache and confusion that come from misinterpreting His words. That's why He joins us in our pilgrimages—He escorts us to eternity—and shows us how to correctly read the Scripture. And He delights in our seeing how everything (even the strange stories of the Old Testament) is ultimately designed to lead us to Him.

If you and I allow Christ to lead us through the genres of Scripture, to guide us through the landscape of hermeneutics, then we can be confident that God will go before us, behind us, and beside us. "Remember," Jesus said, "I am with you always, to the end of the age" (Matt. 28:20).

Pray that God will give you opportunities like Jesus had in Luke 24 to share with others the importance of interpreting the Bible in a way that honors God.

Listening Together

 It all started when my wife and her family rented a beach house for a few weeks in Florida. My plan was simple: I was going to stay on the round plastic float in the ocean for just a few minutes.

After about an hour or so, the soothing rocking of the waves had drifted me to sleep . . . and a hundred yards away from shore. It was the first moment in my life when I have ever felt truly alone.

After a few terrifying seconds, I managed to glimpse a small sliver of land hovering on the horizon. Minutes later, I was safe on shore.

Have you ever felt alone? Maybe you've never fallen asleep in the middle of the ocean, but all of us have experienced feelings of loneliness at one time or another. Perhaps you've just moved to a new community and haven't made any friends yet. Maybe you've experienced the loss of a parent, spouse, or child. None of us are immune to feelings of isolation.

Unlike us, God is never alone. From all eternity, He has existed in three Persons—the Father, the Son, and the Holy Spirit. We call this truth the "Trinity." Make no mistake. God is a personal God, and He has emotions. He experiences regret (Gen. 6:6), anger (Ps. 106:40), jealousy (Exod. 20:5), love (1 John 4:8), and so forth. But not loneliness. And that's why after Christ rose from the dead, He made sure

His disciples would never be alone. "I will not leave you as orphans," He promised (John 14:18). "But the Counselor, the Holy Spirit—the Father will send Him in My name—will teach you all things and remind you of everything I have told you" (v. 26).

You and I were not made to be alone. We were made for life together. Biblical fellowship with other Christians is centered on God's Word. We proclaim God's Word, revere God's Word, and respond to God's Word in repentance.

What are some times that you have felt alone?

Who is your community?

Day 85

The Proclamation of God's Word
Is Central to God's People

"All the people gathered together at the square in front of the Water Gate. They asked Ezra the scribe to bring the book of the law of Moses that the LORD had given Israel. On the first day of the seventh month, Ezra the priest brought the law before the assembly of men, women, and all who could listen with understanding." (*Neh. 8:1–2*)

 According to statistics, the average attention span of an adult is no more than 20 minutes. Due to the rise of fast-paced Internet browsing, television commercials, and other forms of instant gratification media, the number might actually be much lower.

In Nehemiah 8, the Israelites "listened attentively" to the Book of the Law (the Pentateuch) for about six hours, from morning to noon.

Just imagine it. What if your church decided to meet for six hours this Sunday? To us, that might seem like a long time to listen to a Scripture reading. But during the days of Nehemiah, the Jewish exiles couldn't get enough of it.

By 586 BC, the Babylonian Empire had conquered the Southern Kingdom of Judah and had taken God's people

169

into captivity. "By the rivers of Babylon," wrote the psalmist, "there we sat down and wept when we remembered Zion" (Ps. 137:1). It was a difficult season in Israel's history. But God's discipline had finally come to an end. A new day in the history of the Jews had arrived.

When King Cyrus issued an edict allowing the Jews to return to Jerusalem, God's people sought to recover the heritage they had lost in exile. It was time to start rebuilding, to start reforming the walls of the city that had been broken. And central to this reformation was the recovery of Scripture.

In Nehemiah 8:1–12, the word *people* occurs more than ten times. What does this say about the purpose of God's people gathered in worship? Reformation and proclamation always go together. Whenever God starts a genuine reformation in the history of His church, the Holy Scripture always takes front and center stage. In fact, one of the banner cries of the sixteenth-century Protestant Reformation was *sola Scriptura* ("by Scripture alone"). This slogan summarized the authority and centrality of the Holy Scripture against the authority of the pope or of tradition. Sola Scriptura was the idea that God speaks to His people not through leaders or individuals in power but through the Holy Scripture as it is illuminated by the Holy Spirit.

Nehemiah had a working knowledge of sola Scriptura long before Martin Luther nailed his *95 Theses* to a door in 1517. Nehemiah knew that the returning exiles from Babylon could not rebuild their walls and reform their city without hearing a word from the Lord. So when the exiles had settled into their new homes, Ezra, who was a teacher of the law, gathered them together in the square for an appointed time and read to them the ancient words that God had given His people.

We don't know what part of the Law Ezra read. He could have read anything from Genesis, Exodus, Leviticus, Numbers, or Deuteronomy. Perhaps Ezra read to his people the story of Adam and Eve and how humanity's rebellion against God ushered them away from paradise and into the captivity of sin and death. Perhaps Ezra reminded these exiles of Joseph and how his brothers had sold him into slavery but "God planned it for good" (Gen. 50:20). It's possible that Ezra opened the scroll of Exodus and recounted the narrative of how God delivered His people from four hundred years of bondage in Egypt and how He had brought them into the promised land after many years of wandering. All of these stories would have grabbed the attention of these Jews, and for many of them, this might have been the first time they had ever heard the Scriptures actually read out loud.

*How has your hunger for Scripture
changed throughout your walk?*

*In what ways would your relationship with God be
changed if you spent this amount of time in His Word?*

DAY 86

Reading in Light of Eternity

The reading of God's Word reminds us of God's eternal character. It reminds us how we, like the returning exiles, are given the choice either to obey or disobey God. Through the reading of God's Word, we are reminded of our heritage—where we came from and who we are. We are reminded of God's faithfulness to our ancestors and His mighty acts of restoration. But most of all, through the reading of God's Word, we are reminded that God has a master plan, a mission to restore what His people lost—all through the power of the cross of Jesus Christ.

One of the sweetest hopes for Christians is that a day is coming when all forms of captivity will cease—sexual addictions, eating disorders, drug and alcohol abuse, slavery to our own reputations. Death will die, tears will dry up, mourning will turn to morning as God's people bask forever in His glorious presence. But until that day arrives, God has chosen to speak to us through the reading and preaching of His holy Word in the context of biblical community.

In what ways can your church demonstrate the Bible's importance in your fellowship and worship?

DAY 87

God's People Revere God's Word in Posture

"While he was facing the square in front of the Water Gate, he read out of it from daybreak until noon before the men, the women, and those who could understand. All the people listened attentively to the book of the law. Ezra the scribe stood on a high wooden platform made for this purpose. Mattithiah, Shema, Anaiah, Uriah, Hilkiah, and Maaseiah stood beside him on his right; to his left were Pedaiah, Mishael, Malchijah, Hashum, Hash-baddanah, Zechariah, and Meshullam. Ezra opened the book in full view of all the people, since he was elevated above everyone. As he opened it, all the people stood up." Ezra praised the LORD, the great God, and with their hands uplifted all the people said, "Amen, Amen!" Then they bowed down and worshiped the LORD with their faces to the ground." (Neh. 8:3–6)

 If you were an ambassador to Burma in 1867, there was a particular way that you had to approach the king. First, you needed to remove your shoes. Second, you needed to disarm yourself of anything that might be considered a weapon. And third, you would have been required to kneel down and sit on your feet. Failure to abide by these protocols was an offense to the king.

In every culture, the act of kneeling or bowing is virtually always associated with humility. In the East, to kneel in the presence of another is a sign of greeting and respect, much like a handshake or a hug in the West. You and I might not be as familiar with bowing, but during the days of Ezra and Nehemiah, bowing and kneeling were signs of reverence. It was a way to put someone or something above yourself.

That's exactly what the returning Jewish exiles did in Nehemiah 8. They understood that posture mattered. So when the Torah was read, they stood to their feet in attention. Standing for the reading of Scripture was not uncommon in those days (see 9:3). And after the exiles stood for six hours, they all bowed with their faces to the ground to worship God.

Romans 14:11 says, "For it is written: As I live, says the Lord, every knee will bow to Me, and every tongue will give praise to God."

Nehemiah 8 teaches us the importance of elevating Scripture in our lives. It shows us that faith cannot be separated from action. Orthodoxy and orthopraxy go hand in hand, that is to say, what we believe cannot be separated from what we practice. That's why theology matters. That's how the head is connected to the heart. True revival— the kind that comes from God—occurs when Scripture is elevated in our lives. You and I don't have to worry about taking off our shoes in the presence of a Burmese king, but we do have the privilege and opportunity of entering into the presence of the King of kings. And when we do, we'll know, like Moses, that we are standing on holy ground (see Exod. 3).

*How is our posture toward God
evident in the way we live?*

*In what ways can we demonstrate
our reverence for God's Word?*

*Have you ever been in a church service where
people bowed down before God? How about a church
service in which people stood as the Scriptures
were read? What do these physical actions
communicate about our view of the Bible?*

DAY 88

God's People Respond in Repentance and Hold Each Other Accountable

"Jeshua, Bani, Sherebiah, Jamin, Akkub, Shabbethai, Hodiah, Maaseiah, Kelita, Azariah, Jozabad, Hanan, and Pelaiah, who were Levites, explained the law to the people as they stood in their places. They read out of the book of the law of God, translating and giving the meaning so that the people could understand what was read. Nehemiah the governor, Ezra the priest and scribe, and the Levites who were instructing the people said to all of them, "This day is holy to the LORD your God. Do not mourn or weep." For all the people were weeping as they heard the words of the law. Then he said to them, "Go and eat what is rich, drink what is sweet, and send portions to those who have nothing prepared, since today is holy to our Lord. Do not grieve, because the joy of the LORD is your stronghold." And the Levites quieted all the people, saying, "Be still, since today is holy. Do not grieve." Then all the people began to eat and drink, send portions, and have a great celebration, because they had understood the words that were explained to them." (Neh. 8:7–12)

In Nehemiah 8, we learn that there was a "high wooden platform" from which Ezra read the scroll. We could call this a prototype pulpit. We see that because this platform was constructed prior to the worship event, people prepared for this service. Once the Scripture reading got underway, Nehemiah records that the people began raising their hands in the air and shouting, "Amen, Amen!" which affirmed their submission to and agreement with what Ezra was saying.

In Nehemiah's time, the Jews had forgotten some of their Hebrew heritage because they had lived so long in captivity. So after Ezra read the scroll, the priests and scribes and other leaders standing on the platform began to explain the law to the people.

Today, we might call this a sermon—the explanation or exegesis of a passage. Interestingly enough, in Nehemiah's day there were thirteen preachers on stage instead of just one. This suggests there was a system of accountability in the development of their biblical interpretation. No one person was allowed to single-handedly and ultimately decide what God's Word meant for God's people. Instead, a group of leaders and scribes and priests came together to explain the Scriptures.

Translating or explaining the Bible is not just a job for professional translating ministries like Wycliffe Bible Translators. Every pastor, every preacher, every Sunday school teacher, and every disciple-maker also bears this sacred responsibility. In fact, it is the duty of every Christian to ask the questions "How does this Scripture verse relate to my life?" and "How does it relate to my time and culture?" The answers to these questions are not always easy to find. However, we can be confident that every word in the Bible is "profitable for teaching, for rebuking, for correcting, for training in righteousness, so that the man of God may be complete, equipped for every good work" (2 Tim. 3:16–17).

That's what the Jews discovered in Nehemiah 8. The scribes and leaders "read out of the book of the law of God, translating and giving the meaning so that the people could understand what was read." In other words, they explained Scripture. They showed how God's Word was alive and real.

In what ways can a Christian help "translate"
the Bible and make it understandable
for non-Christian friends?

Why is it important to prepare your heart
before hearing the Word proclaimed?

How does initial preparation help us better
hear and apply God's Word to our lives?

Scripture Is the Basis of True Community

And they devoted themselves to the apostles' teaching, to the fellowship, to the breaking of bread, and to the prayers. (Acts 2:42)

During the medieval era in Europe, it was common for a member of a family to draw water from a well or spring near the village. Back in those days, there were no water filters or other purification systems. There were no grocery stores where you could pop in and purchase a liter of Evian or Fiji water. Communities could not function without water, so drawing water from the well was one of the most important jobs in the village. Failure to find a fresh source of drinkable water often resulted in illness.

The Protestant Reformers understood the importance of Scripture in the context of community. They used the phrase *ad fontes* ("to the fountains") to say, "Hey, we don't need popes or religious leaders drawing water for us. We can draw it for ourselves!" And that's exactly what they did. To fulfill that sentiment, Martin Luther translated the Bible into the language of the German people so that everyone could read God's Word.

Long after Ezra read the scroll to the returning exiles of Jerusalem, another event would take place in that city—Pentecost. After Jesus ascended into heaven, the apostle Peter "stood up with the Eleven, raised his voice," and then preached a sermon to a large multitude of Jews from every nation (Acts 2:14). In his sermon, Peter incorporated Old Testament verses such as Joel 2:28–32; Ps. 16:8–11; and Ps. 110:1 to help his audience understand the reason that Jesus Christ had died on the cross and been raised from the dead. After the Word of God was proclaimed, the Jews asked Peter and the other apostles, "Brothers, what must we do?" (Acts 2:37). Peter replied, "Repent . . . and be baptized, each of you, in the name of Jesus Christ for the forgiveness of your sins, and you will receive the gift of the Holy Spirit" (v. 38).

Reverence for the Bible must lead to repentance. There's no sense in revering the Word of God if we are not responding with obedience and faith. Furthermore, Peter understood that without the holy Scriptures, there could be no true Christian community. Peter had been there to hear Jesus say, "Heaven and earth will pass away, but My words will never pass away" (Luke 21:33). Peter watched the Pharisees misquote and twist Scripture when Jesus told them, "You are deceived, because you don't know the Scriptures or the power of God" (Matt. 22:29). Peter knew that the Bible was the fountain—the only uncontaminated source—from which all believers could freely drink. And at Pentecost, approximately three thousand people became followers of Christ that day and were added to the community of faith through baptism. Scripture-based communities always lead us to reach beyond "the group." Why? Because if our communities take seriously the Word of God, they will act on the commands that Christ gives us in His Word, commands such as "Go, therefore, and make disciples of all nations," (Matt. 28:19). And they will hold on to promises such as "Whoever gives just a cup of cold water to one of these little ones because he is a disciple . . . He will never lose his reward!" (10:42). The Bible is always pointing us to Christ. And Christ is always pointing us to others. Therefore, if our communities are biblical, they must also be focused on others.

The apostles' teaching formed the basis for the fellowship of the early church. What can we learn about making disciples from their model?

Go Forth and Spread the Gospel

There is only one time in the whole Bible that God ever felt really alone. It happened on a Friday. Jesus had celebrated the Passover meal with His disciples. He had endured the torments of Gethsemane, the betrayal of Judas, and the trial before Pontius Pilate. Peter had denied Him. His disciples had abandoned Him. And then, after giving His back to the whip and His hands to the nails, Jesus could not keep His pain silent. He screamed, "My God, my God, why have You forsaken Me?" (Matt. 27:46).

Jesus understood why His disciples abandoned Him. Judas wanted money. Peter wanted safety. But God? Why would God the Father leave His Son alone at such a critical moment? Jesus chose to be alone because He wanted you and me to be grafted into the community of faith. He wanted each of us to spend eternity with the God from whom our sins have separated us.

As Christians, we don't have to wait until heaven to experience biblical community. If the Holy Scripture is the foundation of our communities and if we choose to obey Christ's commands to spread His gospel and His love in this world, then we can be confident that God will use our communities to be light and truth in a dark and relativistic society.

Ask God to give you courage and strength to proclaim God's Word to friends, neighbors, and even strangers.